Your 30-DAY JOURNEY —T·O—

Power Over Codependency

C. W. NEAL

OLIVER NELSON

THOMAS NELSON PUBLISHERS
Nashville

Published in Nashville, Tennessee, by Oliver-Nelson Books, a division of Thomas Nelson, Inc., Publishers, and distributed in Canada by Lawson Falle, Ltd., Cambridge, Ontario.

The Bible version used in this publication is THE NEW KING JAMES VERSION. Copyright © 1979, 1980, 1982, Thomas Nelson, Inc., Publishers.

The individuals described in this book are composites of real persons whose identities are disguised to protect their privacy.

Printed in the United States of America.

Library of Congress Cataloging-in-Publication Data
Neal, C.W. (Connie W.), 1958–
    Your 30-day journey to power over codependency / C.W. Neal.
        p.   cm.
    ISBN 0-8407-9627-7
    1. Co-dependence (Psychology)—Treatment. 2. Co-dependence (Psychology)—Problems, exercises, etc. I. Title.
RC569.5.C63N43   1992
616.86—dc20   92-7530
                                                            CIP

1 2 3 4 5 6 — 97 96 95 94 93 92

YOUR 30-DAY JOURNEY
— T·O —

Power Over Codependency

Contents

Introduction

Recovery from an addiction to drugs, alcohol, food, sex, gambling, compulsive spending, and the like seems fairly clear-cut. The addiction gives evidence of being destructive. In contrast, codependency can appear positively saintly as you try to help and take care of everyone else's needs, as you excel and achieve. Precisely, what is recovery from codependency? Is it vowing not to help other people who need you? Is it becoming totally self-sufficient so that you are not dependent on anyone else? Is it recovery from being too nice? If you are not quite sure, this journey is for you. It's fairly easy to tell whether or not someone has relapsed into an addiction. How do you know if you have relapsed into codependency? On your journey you will clearly identify what codependency means in your life and where you draw the line between recovery and relapse.

Codependency is a word coined in the late seventies to describe life patterns commonly identified in people having relationships with alcoholics or other addicts. In essence, codependency describes a life-style where you focus your attention and life energy on controlling others, meeting the needs of others, and trying to change them while neglecting or avoiding aspects of your own life in the process.

The patterns of relating known as codependency are real. However, as with any newly emerging idea, the concept of codependency can be somewhat confusing. You may know enough to make you wonder if codependency is something you need to address in your life. When you hear descriptions of codependent behavior, you may identify with what is being described and recognize that these behavioral theories relate to your life, but you may not be sure how to apply that understanding in practical ways. This journey will show you how to progress from being someone who identifies with codependency issues to someone who has taken steps to gain power over codependency and have confidence that you are walking in recovery.

Being identified as a codependent seems to have become fashionable. Someone else may have given this label to you. It's often assumed that if you are in a close relationship with someone caught up in addictive/compulsive behavior, you must be a codependent, and *you* must change. You might even view being identified as a codependent as guilt by association. If you object to being labeled a codependent, others may smile knowingly since denial is a hallmark of codependency.

The reasoning you may confront goes something like this: "Isn't a codependent someone in relationship with an addict? You are in relationship with an addict; therefore, you must be a codependent." If you follow this line of reasoning to its logical conclusion, the only way to overcome codependency would be for everyone to break off relationship with loved ones whenever they lapse into addictive behavior. If that were the case, no family on earth would be left intact!

Before you try to gain power over codependency,

you need to know exactly what you are confronting. If you don't clearly distinguish the difference between codependent behavior and health-preserving ways of coping, you may end up dismantling positive patterns of life along with negative ones when you take steps to change your life. If you start out believing "I am a codependent," gaining power over codependency will mean changing *who you are*. That can be a trap since one root issue associated with codependency is the belief that there is something intrinsically wrong with who you are. You would be inclined to accept that the solution is to change everything about who you are because that would fit your self-concept.

Recovering from codependency is *not* finding a way to change who you are; it is finding a way to accept who you are while learning to live a life of balanced responsibilities. Trying to change who you are is another manifestation of the false belief that has kept you running around trying to please people, trying to do enough, trying to make people love you, trying to finally earn your place as an acceptable human being. Recovery from codependency involves slowing down enough to look at what drives you to constantly care for the needs of others, while you leave significant needs in your life unattended. Recovery from codependency involves taking your eyes off the crises and demands of the moment so that you can discover what you are avoiding in your life and why you feel compelled to do so.

You are not a codependent. You are a human being who has coped with life as best you knew how. No one develops the life patterns identified as codependency arbitrarily and without good reason. You are most likely a person who, at some time, was overpowered by life's difficulties. Losing yourself in the needs of others was a way you could survive pain that threatened to overwhelm you, and you gained a sense of power and self-worth when you desperately needed both.

If you start your journey with the belief that you are a codependent who needs to change, you will be frustrated in your noble attempts to make yourself over one more time. If you start by accepting that you are a person who reacted to life's traumas by neglecting self-care and your own responsibilities while being consumed in the needs of others, you can find power over codependency without giving up yourself in the process. You can break free of your compulsion to control and rescue others, and you can dare to reclaim a full life for yourself.

When you gain power over codependency, you will be free to help others, but your help will be offered out of real love, not out of the compulsion that says you have to help or else you are worthless. You will be free to say yes and just as free to say no.

This 30-day journey is not a false promise that you can eliminate all codependent behavior patterns in 30 days. You may use this book to conquer codependency in 30 days by discovering that you have been misdiagnosed. You may realize that although you grew up in a dysfunctional family or are married to an alcoholic, you have learned to take responsibility for your own life, and you allow others to do the same with their lives.

There is no miracle one-month cure for a lifetime

of pain and the patterns you developed to cope. However, in the course of 30 days you can come to some basic understandings and take steps that give you power to bring your life into balance. At the end of your journey you will know what a life free of codependency looks like. You will have a clear understanding of your personal boundaries, what you expect of yourself and others, what needs to be done to live a healthy life-style, one day at a time. If you are just beginning to explore these issues, it may take many seasons of healing for you to transform the life patterns identified with codependency. By taking this 30-day journey, you will learn what issues need to be addressed, where to find help, what you can do for yourself, and how to live a full life during your seasons of healing.

Your Commitment to Yourself and Your Journey

If codependency is an issue for you, you will be somewhat uncomfortable focusing attention on your life to the exclusion of others. You may find yourself thinking of all the people you know who could use this book. This journey is not for them. It is for you. You are being challenged to focus on your life, for your own sake, with the same intense energy you have devoted to the lives of others.

Something must have caused you to pick up this book. Something must have caused you to tire of the way you are living. Some crisis, disillusionment, or weariness leads you to ask, Is this all there is to my life? I have given and given of myself, always taking care of others, but what does it get me? What about my needs? What about my life? Those are very good questions. They are questions that draw you toward the kind of life and love you need but may never find if you continue to live as you have.

Codependency is not created in a vacuum. If you have consistently found security in controlling your emotional environment and taking refuge in the lives of other people, there is a reason.

Rich Buhler, a popular radio talk show host, is fond of saying, "If there is debris in your life, that leads one to believe there has probably been devastation." Your current life patterns are, in part, reactions to what has happened in your past and the conclusions you accept about yourself and life as a result.

As a human being, you are created with an instinct for self-preservation. You need security, acceptance, and love just as much as you need air, food, and water. Your emotional needs are not as tangible as physical needs, but they are just as real. Emotional deprivation or injury that leaves you with inner hurts or hungers triggers your self-preservation instinct as powerfully as any physical need.

The following examples show how patterns of behavior can lend clues to what compels codependent behavior. People who feel driven to perform may be responding to a childhood where love was withheld whenever they failed to perform on a grand scale. People who create emotional distance from others may be responding to a previous experience of having a close relationship violated by abuse. People who marry one loser after another may be filling a perceived need. Perhaps they were taught they had no excuse for failure in life. Not having an excuse for imperfection, they marry one!

However, you are not a helpless victim, controlled by the behavior of others. Whatever you experienced, you drew conclusions regarding what the experience meant about you. You decided how to deal with the pain and insecurity. Some people lose themselves in addictions that medicate the pain. They find a substance or mood-altering experience that helps them escape and feel better for a while. The codependent person chooses not to use an addictive substance to alter mood but instead uses relationships. The chosen route of escape is simply staying away from anything that might trigger feelings or insecurities that prove overwhelming. The needs of others seem manageable in comparison to what is wounded within.

Your goal is to gain power over codependency. This diagram depicts the three facets of gaining power over codependency. To the degree you achieve and maintain balance in these three areas, you will experience power over codependency.

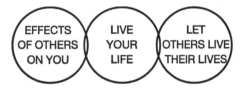

Your recovery plan will include (1) honestly identifying and dealing with the effects the behavior of others has on your life; (2) accepting responsibility for every part of your life, reclaiming the lost parts of life, nourishing yourself in healthy ways, and growing as a whole person; and (3) refraining from diverting attention away from your life by trying to control others and acknowledging boundary lines of another's life and then not trespassing.

PERSONAL EVALUATION

- Are you willing to make this commitment to yourself for your own sake?
- If you are not willing or are hesitant, ask yourself what feelings accompany your unwillingness.
- Anger? (Why should I put in all this work when *they* have the problem?)
- Defensiveness? (Why should I spend my valuable

time looking for clues to a problem I'm not even convinced exists?)
• Fear? (Some things are better left alone.)

ACTION

Your Personal Commitment

I, _____ , am serious about my desire to overcome any life patterns that keep me from living my life to the fullest.

For the next 30 days I am willing to invest the time to read each day's passage and reserve thirty minutes of quiet time to reflect on the issues addressed. I plan to take this time (*circle one*) each morning, lunchtime, afternoon, evening, or before bedtime.

I will honestly consider the personal evaluations, take the action steps (to the best of my ability), and keep a journal of feelings as they emerge. I will share this journey with one person I trust and to whom I will make myself accountable to complete the journey.

I understand that to reach this goal, I must be willing to exercise the courage to look at myself carefully and to endeavor to meet all challenges with perseverance.

I choose to focus attention on my life while refraining from trying to run anyone else's life for the next 30 days. I am willing to move toward truth, even if it is upsetting, and to look back to gain a new perspective from which I can move forward to a better life.

I make this commitment to myself this _____ day of _____, 19 _____ . _____

Signature

Make three sections in your recovery notebook. Label them (1) "Effects," (2) "Live," and (3) "Let Live." In the Effects section you will record how the behavior of others relates to your codependency and how you want to overcome the negative effects. In the Live and Let Live sections, you will clarify relational boundaries and define your relational goals.

REFLECTION

The "Reflection" in each day's journey will suggest topics to consider during your daily quiet time. You may be tempted to skip this part of your journey. You must guard your quiet time as if your recovery depended on it. You must stop all the busyness (talking, writing, obsessing about what you have to do or what someone else may be doing, and so on) so that you can catch a glimpse of what you are avoiding in your life.

Make arrangements to be alone and undisturbed. If feelings arise, try to accept them and allow yourself to feel them. You may want to write out the feelings or memories but for the most part avoid doing anything other than reflecting. If you feel overwhelmed, contact someone who can help you deal with the roots of your overwhelming emotions.

ENCOURAGEMENT

The same innate coping abilities that helped you distance yourself from parts of life that were too painful to bear can now help you reclaim your life and gain power over codependency.

FOOD FOR THOUGHT

Delusions are like a roomful of noisy acquaintances; they keep you from being alone with the truth.

—Marian J. Thomas

The Tree of Your Life

The life of a codependent person can be represented by a tree. This tree is beautiful. Its great branches stretch toward the sky, providing shade for anyone who would like to rest beneath it. The dense foliage is filled with sounds of birds, squirrels, woodpeckers, and a host of insects that make their home amidst the branches and in every available knothole. No one seems to notice that the soil in which the tree is planted has not been tilled or cultivated in ever so long. The roots are stunted; the soil is depleted. Very little nourishment can get through to replenish the life of the tree. The tree takes care of everyone, but no one takes care of the tree. It seems fine. The beauty, the busyness in the branches, and the coolness of the shade—all draw attention away from the tree, which is slowly wasting away from within.

The branches represent areas where you extend yourself into the lives of others. The trunk represents your personal life and inner life. The roots represent your past experiences, beliefs about yourself, and feelings buried in the soil of your past.

A common element of codependency is the need to be socially acceptable at all costs in order to feel O.K. You may cover up embarrassing circumstances, protect someone from the consequences of personal behavior, lie, or deny real problems. These actions enable an addict, abuser, or other dependent person to continue the destructive life-style without taking responsibility. These actions also protect your image and give you a sense of control and momentary security.

Not all codependency involves direct denial and enabling behavior. You may simply neglect yourself and be driven to perform. If you doubt your value as a human being, you may find comfort by making yourself available at any hour of the day or night to meet the needs of others. As John Bradshaw so aptly put it, "You become a human doing instead of a human being." You may struggle with guilt whenever you rest, whenever you say no to a request, or whenever you do something only for yourself.

If you avoid those things in life that trigger overwhelming memories and feelings at the root of who you are, you leave parts of your past untouched, the soil untilled. You say things like, "What's past is past; there's no good done in dredging it up." But the past is not really past if you avoid parts of life today to protect yourself. Avoidance of issues and repression of feelings cut you off from a range of feelings, memories, and activities in your day-to-day life.

Unresolved traumas and losses will powerfully emerge in some form. The adult child of an alcoholic may marry an alcoholic and try to save the spouse the way the person tried to save the alcoholic parent. The person sexually abused as a child may avoid sex altogether by becoming overweight or may display a lack of self-care by becoming indiscriminate about sexual partners. Either way the person has cut off the real intimacy of sex in marriage as it was intended. Another person may refuse to acknowledge a certain holiday because of the death of a loved one at that time of year. Another person may have no conscious memory of past trauma but may experience unexplained physical ailments that act as body clues to the pain of the past.

It's understandable that you would want to numb yourself to the chance of being hurt again. However, this way of dealing with your past shows that the past is not over for you. You feel compelled to maintain your defenses against it without realizing that you are giving up a part of yourself in the process.

As your tree of life continues to grow, the telling moment comes when you must make a choice: Do you dislodge those who have nested there and prune the branches to sustain continued health of the tree? Pruning represents cutting back on the control and care of others enough to give you a chance to replenish your needs. If you are codependent, you forgo pruning for the sake of the nesters. There is no limit to what you are willing to give or endure for the sake of others. You do not sacrifice yourself out of love freely given. Your value, relationships, and security are based on being a nesting place for others. Your identity is the rescuer, savior, martyr, or one who holds things together for everyone else. Perhaps you don't believe the tree deserves a place in the world apart from its usefulness and appearance. Perhaps you fear that if you let go of controlling, manipulating, rescuing, and doing more than enough, the people you love would leave you.

The understanding of what compels you in these ways is probably hidden in the soil of your past, usually your early years of life. Something buried there holds the key to why you focus much of your energy toward others and away from yourself.

PERSONAL EVALUATION

- Who is dependent upon you emotionally, financially, and in other ways?
- Who do you try to control, manipulate, rescue, fix, or change?
- Does your life appear to be fine, but you sometimes feel empty inside and wonder if anyone knows the real you?
- How often does your involvement in the lives of others leave you feeling used or depleted?
- Do you feel uncomfortable receiving help, compliments, good sensations, and other nourishing experiences?
- On a regular basis, what do you do for yourself that rejuvenates you (rest, fun, creative expression, and so on)?

ACTION

Draw a picture of what the tree of your life looks like.

Make the size of *the branches* proportionate to your involvement in the lives of others and how much of your life is focused away from yourself. (This can represent giving of yourself to many people or the degree to which you involve your life with one person.) Write in the names of your "nesters."

Make the thickness and appearance of *the trunk* relate to how you secretly feel in terms of personal fulfillment.

Make *the roots* reach out and appear healthy to the degree that you feel you are receiving nourishment for your personal and inner life. If you know of a particular feeling, past experience, or issue that you have made off-limits, label that root and darken it.

REFLECTION

Spend your quiet time reflecting on each area of your life designated by the branches, trunk, and roots. Allow yourself to feel whatever feelings arise.

ENCOURAGEMENT

The roots you may not want to get near may be the channel through which new life is vitalized.

Gaining Power, Not Just Understanding

The purpose of this book is not so much to help you understand codependency as it is to encourage action that will give you power over it.

Let's say you desire to build a house for your family, and you spend all your time reading about styles of houses, building materials, floor plans, and options for landscaping, roofing, plumbing, and so on. You would understand a great deal about building houses, but you would be no closer to having one built to suit the needs of your family. You need blueprints to get started.

The same is true of gaining power over codependency. If you diligently studied every book available, attended meetings, learned the jargon, and talked about wanting to be free of codependency, yet never determined precisely how codependency manifests in your life and what your specific goals are to gain power over your codependent behavior, you would be no closer to reaching your desired result.

Here is what you will do to gain power over codependency. First, you will define your issues in these categories:

- How is your life negatively affected by the behavior of others?
- What do you need to reclaim and take responsibility for in your life to experience wholeness?

- Where do you overstep the boundaries into the lives of others (controlling, fixing, trying to change, taking responsibility for them, manipulating, and so on)?

Second, you will envision what life can be like when you resolve the effects the lives of others have had on you, when you are freely living your life and releasing others to live their lives. In doing this, you will identify benefits that will motivate you to persevere.

Third, you will clearly identify obstacles and injuries that keep you from gaining power over codependency.

Fourth, you will break down the vague general problem, known as codependency, into smaller, more manageable problems; then you will solve each problem individually, after determining an appropriate course of action and the order of importance to you.

Fifth, you will decide where to turn for the help you need.

Sixth, you will commit yourself to a new order of priorities (you choose for yourself), which allow you to live within the boundaries of recovery.

Seventh, you will schedule these commitments into your daily life and establish a system of checks and balances to keep you on track.

Eighth, once you have established a new order in your life, you will practice reviewing your commitment daily to ensure against falling back into old patterns of codependency, and to expand and adapt your life plans as you grow beyond recovery.

Ninth, when you successfully overcome obstacles and experience healing of your injuries that were top priorities, you choose which obstacles and injuries to focus on next.

PERSONAL EVALUATION

- Do you understand codependency in general terms or in specific terms as it applies to your life?
- Do you have a clear mental picture of what life will be like when you have power over codependency and what life will be like twenty years from now if you do not?
- Once you have established a new order in your life, are you willing to take a few moments each day to maintain order?

ACTION

Think of a time when you made a commitment that required a new order in your life. (An example would be getting married or having a child, then changing your life-style to accommodate your commitment to the other person, or even taking on a new job or hobby that required juggling your life-style to be able to do what you wanted to do.)

Write a description of this experience beginning with this sentence: "I was able to change my life in keeping with an important new commitment when I . . ."

REFLECTION

Recall the satisfaction you gained from being able to change your life in the way you just described Think about what you had to do, the energy you expended, the obstacles you overcame. Chances are that your selection was something you did for someone else. Helping others seems to come easier for those who deal with codependency than doing something to help themselves. Now, reflect on a time when you did something just for you to change your life for the better, even if it was a small step. Does it seem more difficult to make changes that are just to help you?

ENCOURAGEMENT

The same strength of character, determination, skills, energy, and industriousness that you have used in helping and taking care of others are at your disposal for dealing with your issues. You have the tools; you simply need to use them on your own behalf.

FOOD FOR THOUGHT

Real optimism knows about difficulties but believes they can be overcome.
—William Arthur Ward

What's at Stake?

Codependent behavior was originally the lifesaver you clung to in the storms of life. The coping mechanisms served you well in times when you had to survive. Unless you become very clear about the positive benefits you will experience when you abandon your codependent way of life, you will not want to change. Today you will envision the benefits of gaining power over codependency. This positive motivation will help you complete your transforming journey.

Living to accommodate and please others, hiding your true self in an attempt to manage the lives around you, gets in the way of love. You give of yourself beyond the call of duty, concluding that after all you have done for others, they will be obligated to give back to you or love you. However, human nature recoils from such pressure and manipulation. You don't get back what you feel is owed, and you resent the lack. You eventually end up feeling angry because your giving is unappreciated and taken for granted.

When expressions of love are offered to you, you may discount them and not be able to receive the real love within your reach. First, since you feel love is owed, you accept it not as an expression of the heart but as a response born of obligation. The fact that you manipulated their response takes away the joy of being loved. Second, any love you receive is suspect. Since you have revealed only what you think will please people or what you needed to reveal to get your way, the love coming to you is being directed to the image you project, not the real you.

Sometimes others will resist your manipulations, refusing to be forced to show love. When this power struggle ensues, your resentment of their failure to express the love you feel is owed, in the way you deem appropriate, may prompt you to try to control the others more to make them love you. This type of relational struggle can go on for years, with one incident building on another. Whether the others finally give in and show you the expression of love you require or not, you lose. Love on demand is slavery, not love. You may finally get what you demand and yet be no closer to receiving the love you desperately crave.

Overcoming codependency lets you experience love in greater measure. When you dare to stop keeping emotional accounts of the love owed for all you do and you choose to express love with no strings attached, without trying to manipulate a loving response, you open the door to true love.

When you spend your life taking care of everyone and everything other than yourself, people see you as the strong one who has no needs or wants. They learn, at your knee, to rely on you. They never know your needs, or that you even have any, because you never display your needs. The relationship is not set up for them to give to you. Should you ever become exhausted or otherwise decide to stop being the supplier of their needs, they will leave to find someone who will take care of them the way you used to. If they grow and their needs change, they will find someone else to meet those needs; and if your relationship did not involve a free flow of giving and receiving, you may find yourself cut off from those for whom you sacrificed your life.

Part of gaining power over codependency involves developing relationships with some people who do not need you but love you anyway. It also involves transforming relationships with those you used to rescue into healthier relationships between equals. You may lose some relationships founded solely on your performance and what you can do for the other party, but that will only be a revelation of what is true. If you face that truth now and diversify your relationships, you will be able to live with the loss of a few relationships while gaining support from new ones.

Gaining power over codependency means taking responsibility for your choices about who you give yourself to, what you sacrifice in the process, and accepting the consequences of those choices. It means letting go of blaming anyone but yourself for your lack of fulfillment and happiness. When you dare to live your life while shouldering the responsibility for your happiness, you will be free to experience a full range of joyous emotions, peace, serenity, self-respect, adventure, fun, and deep satisfaction. Remaining stuck in your codependent relationships leads to being stressed, angry, resentful, bitter, isolated, frustrated, and confused.

PERSONAL EVALUATION

- Do you want more out of life than you're getting?
- Do you believe that the world would suffer loss if you abdicated living your life and expressing yourself fully?
- When have you discounted love because you felt it was born of obligation or because people didn't know the real you?
- When have you tried to manipulate someone into showing you love? How did the relationship work out?
- When you begin to change your codependent lifestyle, which relationships do you suspect will continue, which will be transformed, and which will be lost?
- To what degree are you already becoming stressed, angry, resentful, bitter, isolated, frustrated, and confused? How do these feelings relate to codependent life patterns?

ACTION

Make a list of all the possible benefits you will receive from gaining power over codependency. Include the things you want out of life that you have not yet pursued because of being caught up in the lives of others.

Make another list of what you fear may happen or may be lost if you let go of your codependent ways of relating.

REFLECTION

Fear plays a significant role in creating codependent behavior (fear of being rejected, being deemed unlovable, being abandoned, experiencing the kind of pain you've known in the past, disappointing someone, and so on). As you consider the benefits of having power over codependency and your fear of loss, how does the hope of a better way of life weigh out against your fears?

Allow yourself to feel the fear; be aware of any memories of other experiences prompted by these feelings. Allow yourself to feel the hope of being free to live your life and pursue your desires and dreams.

ENCOURAGEMENT

You have a right to hope to live your life in a rewarding way. Hold on to the hope. It will give you a great source of power for your journey.

FOOD FOR THOUGHT

Struggling with all your might to survive is quite different from choosing to live your life to the fullest.

Pruning Back Codependent Behaviors

Anyone who has worked with addicts knows that it is impossible to recover, or to even get to the real issues of life, if the person is still using the addictive substance. The alcoholic must stop drinking alcohol. The drug addict must stop drug use. The compulsive gambler must stop wagering. With these addictions it is easy to see what must be done to begin recovery.

Some people become addicted to substances or experiences, such as food, sex, work, or religion, that are in themselves healthy, but the individuals use them in inappropriate ways. When the misuse or excessive use of something good becomes addictive, sobriety is measured by bringing those good things back into the range of appropriate use.

In these instances it is not as clear what must be cut out for recovery to begin. The person who is a compulsive overeater need not stop eating; the sex addict need not become celibate; the workaholic need not quit the job. However, for recovery to begin, each one must identify and eliminate all excessive and inappropriate use of what has become the form of addiction. To conquer codependency, you must identify and cut back on certain relational patterns that are inappropriate and activities and involvements that act as an escape from your life.

Don't try to do this alone. Get feedback from someone who knows you and is supportive of your journey. A professional counselor would be best. If that is not possible, a caring friend or a member of Codependents Anonymous or another related support group will suffice. The person can help you see through any self-protective blind spots.

Here are some guidelines to help you determine where you need to cut back:

- Take responsibility only for your actions and those of your minor children.
- Do not carry the burden or responsibility for others' problems or consequences of their choices.
- Do not cover up for or lie on behalf of others to protect them from the consequences of their actions.
- At work, pare back to doing what is called for in your assigned job description, without jeopardizing your job security.
- Relieve yourself of all nonessential extracurricular involvements for this month. Do what you can to postpone any pressing deadlines.
- Excuse yourself from family expectations (within your extended family) by explaining that you are in the process of dealing with some significant personal issues.

If you find it impossible to take your mind off others or to limit your focus to your life even for a brief time, I suggest that you consider seeking the help of professionals who can assist you in cutting back enough to begin recovery.

Personal Evaluation

Answer these questions. Exclude involvement in your life or the lives of your minor children (these are generally appropriate involvements).

- Whose problems are you currently worrying about?
- Whose life do you currently feel responsible to try to change, fix, control, or rescue from the consequences of personal behavior?
- Who actively needs your help at this season of time (include groups that ask for or expect your help)?
- What are your current commitments (at home, work, or school; with friends; social events; and volunteer activities)?
- What routine duties do immediate family and extended family members expect of you?

Action

List your current worries on a sheet of paper. Seal the list in an envelope, and make a choice to leave the worries alone until you have completed your journey. If you like, you can pick them back up and take them on yourself again at that time.

Compose a list of persons you currently feel responsible for (excepting minor children). Notify them that they will have to get by for a month without your help and make other arrangements as warranted.

Communicate with individuals and groups that currently need your help. Explain that you have some other important things you need to do this month. In most cases they can find someone else to help or wait for 30 days until you are available. Excuse yourself for the time being.

Contact those people and groups to whom you have made commitments. Ask them if you can be temporarily relieved of your obligations or if you can reduce them significantly during this 30-day journey. Negotiate whatever arrangements you can without breaking your commitments.

If you are married, talk this step over with your spouse. You are not going to take a vacation from fulfilling your role in the family, but your change in focus will have an impact. Let your immediate family know that the focus of your attention will be more introspective than usual so that they don't misinterpret your change in behavior. Ask for their help in allowing you the time and solitude you need to go through each day's journey.

Communicate with members of your extended family who have expectations of you. Let them know, lovingly but firmly, that they can't expect much from you for the next month or so. Explain only as much as you feel comfortable discussing. Refrain from trying to get their approval for your journey.

REFLECTION

You may be thinking, *There's no way! I can't do that.* That is probably pretty close to the way alcoholics feel when they are told that they must stop drinking to begin recovery. Consider the parallel and its implications for your life.

ENCOURAGEMENT

You can take the steps in today's journey, even though you may feel resistance at every point. This temporary discomfort is for your ultimate well-being. Remember, the purpose of all pruning is for you to become better nourished, healthier, and more productive in the future. Even Jesus Christ recommended occasional times of pruning and cited the reason. He told His disciples: "I am the true vine, and My Father is the vinedresser. Every branch in Me that does not bear fruit He takes away; and every branch that bears fruit He prunes, that it may bear more fruit" (John 15:1–2).

FOOD FOR THOUGHT

You will not die from sobriety.
—Anonymous

The Focus of Your Recovery Is You

Emily entered an inpatient treatment program for depression after discovering that her "perfect" husband struggled with sex addiction and had been involved in pornography, numerous affairs, and indiscriminate sexual encounters. She didn't consider herself depressed, but if that's what they wanted to call her, she would go along with it. What she really wanted to do was gain insight into helping her husband. He was the one with the problem. She was obsessed with understanding what could cause such behavior, discovering how she could make sure he never acted out again, and finding out if his compulsive behavior was her fault.

The first few days in the hospital she struggled with the thought that maybe there was something wrong with her. Surely, if she had been a good enough wife, this wouldn't have happened. That is what people had intimated. Maybe she wasn't attractive enough. Maybe she wasn't adventurous enough sexually. She saw herself as intricately connected with his problem. She saw herself as both the cause and the cure. She didn't consider ending the relationship. She couldn't conceive of living without him. Anyway, this situation could work to her advantage. If she stood by him and helped him get through this problem, he would never dare to leave her.

The therapist asked Emily to talk about herself.

At first she recounted her qualifications and achievements as though she were interviewing for a job or trying to favorably impress a date. "What about the painful areas of your life before this crisis?" asked the doctor. "Tell me about you and your life history. Especially highlight the parts you don't like to talk about."

"Oh, that," Emily quietly replied. With a frozen expression on her face she blandly recounted a series of traumatic experiences within her family of origin: adultery, death threats, suicide attempts, alcoholism, drug abuse, physical violence, poverty, imprisonments, untimely deaths, abandonments, compulsive gambling, overdoses, attempted murders, and incest.

In treatment Emily learned to deal with her feelings related to what her husband had done. She came to accept that his addiction was his problem and his recovery was his domain. She made a commitment to let go of all the manipulations she used to guarantee his dependence upon her, choosing to stay in the relationship out of love rather than fear.

She also was safely guided in dealing with the emotional debris of her life. As the therapists helped her face the feelings that seemed too much to bear, she began to see patterns in her life, to understand that she transferred attention away from herself as a means of coping and established relationships with people who seemed to need her strength so that she could manipulate and control. She realized that she scouted for neediness in others as an opportunity to tie them to her. In that way she lessened the possibility of being abandoned as she had been as a child. Her desperate fear of abandonment made relationships based on being needed a "safe" substitute for the risk of real love.

She was led to consider parts of normal day-to-day life that were overlooked and to notice areas of her life that she either refused to take responsibility for or felt emotionally unable to handle. She had constructed a life where there wasn't enough time or emotional energy to deal with her issues. Besides, they paled in comparison to the needs and problems of others, which is precisely why she gravitated toward a career and relationships that surrounded her with needy people.

Your overinvolvement in the lives of others is a smoke screen to conceal an overwhelming amount of pain and self-doubt. Recovery lies not in analyzing the smoke but in clearing it away so that you can look more carefully at your life, especially life before current relationships or crises took center stage.

PERSONAL EVALUATION

- When did you *first* become consumed with thinking about another person's behavior: how you could change it, what you could do to control it, or what you may have done to cause it?
- What was your life like during that time?
- When you recount understandably painful events that happened in your life, are you disconnected from your emotions?
- Do you have blank spots in your memory, spans of time you cannot recall?
- Do you have selective memory, able to recall

only positive experiences when you suspect there is more to the story?

- When have you justified neglecting or avoiding your problems and responsibilities because they seemed small in comparison to the problems and needs of others?
- When have you kept account of wrongs you suffered and the way you supported others in their times of need as an emotional insurance policy to bind them to you for life?

ACTION

List three living conditions or events in your history that would understandably cause difficult emotions, which you recall with little or no emotion.

List three problem areas in your life that you minimized or ignored while you focused your attention on others.

List three ways you involve yourself in the lives of others while your issues go unattended.

REFLECTION

Consider what elements of the story about Emily parallel your thoughts and feelings about yourself and persons you are trying to control, fix, or change. How do you feel when you move closer to dealing with issues in your life?

ENCOURAGEMENT

Acknowledging that problems exist in your life and accepting the challenge to focus on yourself mean that you are taking a step toward gaining power over codependency. You are well on your way toward a better life, even if others never change.

FOOD FOR THOUGHT

Why do you look at the speck in your brother's eye, but do not consider the plank in your own eye? Or how can you say to your brother, "Let me remove the speck from your eye"; and look, a plank is in your own eye? Hypocrite! First remove the plank from your own eye, and then you will see clearly to remove the speck from your brother's eye.

—Jesus Christ

Whose Tune Do You Sing To?

One characteristic common to codependency is living life directed by external cues rather than internal cues. That way of life needs to be corrected to gain power over codependency. The following illustration may help you identify that type of behavior in your life.

Suppose you joined a choir because you wanted to sing and perform. The proper way to prepare is to learn your part as the notes, rhythm, melody, and harmony are written. But let's suppose that you joined the choir and began performing without ever having heard the music and without ever having learned your part. In fact, suppose you don't know how voices blend together to create harmony. Nevertheless, you are thrilled to be a part of the choir, and you sing out enthusiastically. But you don't sing the right notes. And you get an immediate response from those around you. The choristers stare at you. "You're off key," one whispers. "Sing higher!" another says. You try to sing higher. After a few adjustments of pitch, the critical looks of the others melt into expressions of relief. After a while you develop the ability to adjust your singing to the silent glances and hand motions of those around you. Sometimes, because you fear rejection, you move your lips without making a sound. You learn that whenever you want to sing, you must sing according to the dictates of others.

In this example, singing can represent your desire to live to your full potential and to be accepted and the choir can represent your family of origin. Someone in your family should have helped you learn a healthy way to live, defined by set values, moral guidelines, and life-giving principles.

If your family was dysfunctional, however, you may not have been informed that there was any other way to live. You may always have had the desire to sing the song of life, but you may not have known the tune and may not have believed you had the capacity to learn. The only way you learned to live was by changing your performance in response to the reactions of those in your family.

Your survival may have depended on your ability to read the cues of those around you and adjust your behavior until their disapproval was appeased. Sometimes that may have meant you didn't sing the song of life at all, that you just went through the motions, pretending to be what you thought they wanted you to be.

If you grew up in a closed or repressive family system, your family may not have been able to lead you into a healthy life because of their own problems. Instead of freeing you to express yourself, their rules may have stifled the true expression of your feelings, thoughts, opinions, desires, perceptions, and talents. The way you learned to survive in your family of origin isn't necessarily the way to live a healthy life. This realization gives you the opportunity to grasp the joy of living that has been stifled.

PERSONAL EVALUATION

Do you see yourself being directed externally by others or directed internally by your values and principles?

In your family of origin, what may have influenced you to live according to the reactions of others, rather than developing your own abilities to live from within?

Can you think of anything (an experience or something you were told) that convinced you that you lack abilities needed to live a fulfilling life?

What specific abilities do you doubt most in yourself (the ability to think, choose, be attractive, excel, learn, support yourself, maintain a relationship, and so on)?

ACTION

On a scale of one to ten, rate the degree to which you were controlled by trying to please or appease others as a child, and again for how you live your life now. One would be completely directed by external cues, five would be half internally directed and half externally directed, and ten would be totally internally directed without regard for the cues coming from others.

List the names of those in your childhood "choir" (those for whom you adjusted your lifestyle in order to please or appease).

List the names of those you currently try to please or appease.

List the names of those you look to as examples of how to live a healthy life.

REFLECTION

In this life no one sings solo; you really are part of a larger group. The goal is to learn to carry your part, even though those around you may not. You may find your response to an oppressive family "choir" was to aim for complete independence. Consider how well you are able to blend your life with others using internal cues.

ENCOURAGEMENT

The tune of life is something you can learn. There is a great sense of freedom and confidence to be enjoyed once you learn the tune and find courage to sing out with all your heart.

FOOD FOR THOUGHT

If you do not live the life you believe, you will believe the life you live.

—Zig Ziglar

The Missing Pieces Hold
the Clues

Somewhere inside you is a collection of memories, feelings, pleasures, hopes, and dreams that has been lost to you. Dealing with certain areas of life triggers fearful emotions, reminds you of your stormy past, or stirs up feelings that life is dangerously out of control. You don't make a conscious choice to shut off those feelings or refuse to deal with those areas of life. You just avoid them.

Here's an example. Ralph's father was a compulsive gambler. Ralph grew up hearing promises of a bright future with lots of money. Each time Daddy left for the race track, he said, "If I win today, I'll bring you a present," or "When we hit it big, we can have a big house, and maybe we can get you a pony."

In real life there was never enough money to pay the bills. The phone was disconnected. As a teenager, Ralph used the phone booth to call friends and made up excuses to cover his shame. Creditors were at the door. Daddy made Ralph tell them he wasn't home. When the school year began, they couldn't afford new clothes, so Ralph made the best of what he could find at a thrift store. The family eventually lost their modest home, and when Daddy died, they borrowed money to bury him.

It's not clear when it happened, but at some time Ralph tossed away hopes of financial security. As an adult, he became successful in his career, but he refused to deal with financial matters. Sometimes bills weren't paid because he avoided looking at them. His wife usually handled the money. Thinking about money, either having it or not having it, made him uncomfortable so he abandoned that part of his life. It took a crisis—a financial collapse coupled with seeing his own children begin to worry over financial insecurity—before Ralph would face that part of his life.

Anything that brings you back to the lost areas of yourself may be tremendously intimidating, but it offers you a wonderful opportunity to reclaim your life and realize that you can handle uncomfortable issues, one by one.

PERSONAL EVALUATION

- Do you have any idea what is in the abandoned corners of your soul?
- What is there about your life (past and present) that you don't want to think about or talk about?

ACTION

List anything you are aware of that is missing from your life, holding you back from a whole and satisfying life.

Rephrase your list into a list of things you would want (if you allowed yourself to want) to make your life fulfilling.

REFLECTION

Doing this exercise may arouse buried emotions. What are the feelings associated with each item you listed? If you are angry, does the anger protect you from the more overwhelming feelings of fear and sadness? Do you feel any desperation at the thought of dealing with these issues that you have avoided for so long? Was it hard to turn your deficits into desires?

ENCOURAGEMENT

You can successfully reclaim each lost area of your life and have a fresh start. You can face whatever troubling emotions are associated with those elements of life, take responsibility for your life, and enjoy the benefits.

FOOD FOR THOUGHT

It is never too late to be what you might have been.

—George Eliot

Physical Life

Areas of everyday life that would normally be non-threatening can become associated with danger or emotional pain. When this happens, your self-preservation instinct warns you to stay away from whatever you have associated with further danger. Things that would normally elicit no particular response become flares marking where a painful experience has occurred and directing you to detour around the debris of whatever caused your pain.

You are now going to undertake a portion of your journey where you will sort out for yourself precisely what you are avoiding in your life and what this emotional debris points to that needs to be cleared up. You will take specific areas of life one at a time.

PERSONAL EVALUATION

The first area you will consider is your physical life. Go over these lists of items that are accepted as part of normal behavior to take care of life on a physical plane. Rate on a scale of one to ten how well you care for yourself in these ways. (One would be not caring for yourself at all in these ways; ten would be consistent self-care.)

If there is a general category listed and you can identify a particular action you neglect, be as specific as you possibly can. For example, where the

list reads, "Take medication as prescribed by doctor," and you consistently allow yourself to run out
of prescription medication without getting the necessary refills, note the specific behavior. Place a
check next to any area of physical self-care that you
do not perform on a regular basis. (Note: You will
probably find these lists ridiculously obvious. However, that is precisely the point. When something
prevents you from caring for your life in a basic
way, it possibly indicates something more than
what appears on the surface.)

Health and Safety   *Rating*
1. Maintain a safe environment at home, work, and play. . . ____
2. Obey safety rules at home, work, and play. . . . . ____
3. Protect yourself from those who would do you harm. . .   ____
4. Learn and practice self-protection skills relative to the
   level of danger in your environment. . . . . ____
5. Practice preventive medical care on a regular basis (annual
   medical checkup, following doctor's instructions). . . . . ____
6. Practice preventive dental care on a regular basis (checkup
   every six months). . . . . ____
7. Protect your sexual boundaries. See yourself as a sexual
   person designed for meaningful relationship rather than a
   sexual object to be used to satisfy someone else's sexual
   desires. . . . . ____
8. Eat a healthy and balanced diet. . . . . ____
9. Allow yourself enough privacy to maintain dignity. . . . . ____
10. Allow yourself needed amounts of rest to maintain peak
    performance (approximately eight hours of sleep nightly,
    quiet times while awake, one day of rest each week, annual
    vacations). . . . . ____
11. Follow routine care for maintaining the health of *each part*
    of your body. (For example, if you wear contact lenses, do
    you regularly clean, disinfect, and care for them as directed
    to protect your eyes from possible health risks? If you work
    on your feet, do you provide yourself with proper footwear
    to give your feet support and protection from injury?) . . . ____

12. Trace down unexplained chronic physical conditions. (These are sometimes physical clues to repressed trauma.) _____
13. Take medication as prescribed by doctor. . . . . _____
14. Care for personal hygiene as appropriate for your physical condition. Attend to any physical problems or health problems related to your sex organs. (This point is cited because treating your sex organs differently from the way you treat other parts of your body may indicate some sort of abuse.) . . . . _____
15. Exercise aerobically to develop strength and coordination. _____
16. Keep your living space reasonably clean and orderly. . . _____
17. Enjoy the full use of all your senses without isolating yourself from some facet of life: hearing, smelling, tasting, touching, seeing, and enjoying your sexuality. . . . . _____
18. Satisfy your appetite for food and drink regularly in healthy ways rather than live in a cycle of self-deprivation, binges, and guilt. . . . . _____

Physical Grooming   *Rating*
1. Shower or bathe daily. _____
2. Wash your hands before eating and after using the bathroom. . . . . _____
3. Style and groom hair attractively every day. . . . . _____
4. Wash your hair regularly to maintain a well groomed appearance. . . . . _____
5. Brush teeth two to three times daily; floss daily. . . . . . _____
6. Groom fingernails and toenails regularly. . . . . _____
7. Provide yourself with clothing appropriate to the climate and socially acceptable, depending on the occasion. . . . _____
8. Wear clothing that is neat and clean every day. . . . . . . _____
9. Women: wear cosmetics if you choose. . . . . _____
10. Treat yourself to little extras that enhance your appearance and make you feel better about yourself, such as accessories, jewelry, manicures, facials, and so on. . . . . _____

Environment and Possessions   *Rating*
1. Buy yourself clothing as needed: outerwear, casual wear, work attire, shoes, socks and underwear, sleepwear and lingerie, special occasion clothes, coordinated accessories, and so on. (Note if you feel more comfortable buying

these items for others in your family than you do for your-self, and specify any particular items of clothing you don't buy for yourself.) . . . .   ——

2. Care for clothing in a responsible manner: regular launder-ing, mending, pressing, hanging up in closet, and so on.   ——

3. Create a home environment that provides for your particu-lar needs and the needs of your family. . . . .   ——

4. Establish routine to maintain home environment you have created: make beds upon rising, wash dishes, vacuum floors as needed, dust furniture, present meals attractively at regular times, have each room of your home cleaned on a regular schedule (daily, weekly, semiannually, or annually as needed), plan and provide food for meals, have utilities continually working, and so on. (Note any particular areas of home care that cause you to procrastinate or feel ashamed when you think about them.) . . . .   ——

5. Establish and enforce boundaries that maintain the safety, beauty, order, and comfort of your home to meet the needs of your family. (This category includes not tolerating vio-lence, substance abuse, and other out-of-control behavior in your home. Also, limit your commitments so that you can take enough time at home with your family to meet one another's legitimate needs.) . . . .   ——

6. Create and maintain a work or school environment that serves your needs and is orderly and attractive. . . . . .   ——

7. Buy things that appeal to your senses in a positive way: fragrances for body and home, music, artwork, interior decorating items, foods and drinks you love, soft fabrics that are nice to the touch, and so on. . . . .   ——

8. Take responsibility for maintaining your possessions. (For example, do you keep your car clean inside and out? Do you read the manuals for appliances and take care of them as instructed?) . . . .   ——

9. Get repairs whenever something you own breaks or is damaged. . . . .   ——

ACTION

For all the items you rated at five or lower, you will also write a letter in the margin to designate the following: an *N* if this is something you neglect; an *A* if this is something you avoid; an *R* if this is something you refuse to take responsibility for; a *C* if this is not something missing but something you rigidly control. Be as specific and honest as possible.

Here is how to determine which category applies. Place it in the *N* (neglected) category if it doesn't seem important but holds no emotional intensity when you think about it. It just isn't a priority. Place it in the *A* (avoided) category if it is something you feel uncomfortable with or procrastinate over, or it holds some level of emotional intensity. Place it in the *R* (refused) category if it is something you have thought about and acknowledge that it should be accepted as your responsibility but, for some reason, have exempted yourself from taking responsibility. Place an item in the *C* (rigidly controlled) category if you feel a sense of compulsion over that area of life, such as feeling driven to keep your home spotless, compulsively washing your hands, being unwilling to allow your children to grow up and assume their own lives, and so on.

REFLECTION

Consider what patterns you notice related to taking care of yourself physically. Think about anything in your upbringing or experience that might affect the areas where you do not take care of yourself or where you feel compelled to exert rigid controls. Theorize about why you neglect or control these areas.

ENCOURAGEMENT

These are pieces of a puzzle. As you sort through them, you will begin to see what areas of your life need to be reclaimed and why you have chosen to leave some areas untouched. You will gain power over codependency as you choose areas of life to reclaim for your own well-being.

FOOD FOR THOUGHT

Confrontation doesn't always bring a solution to the problem, but until you confront the problem, there will be no solution.

—James Baldwin

Emotional Life

Emotions can appear as formidable enemies when you are living in a situation that is out of control, especially if you experienced it as a child. Feelings of powerlessness, deep shame, abandonment, foreboding, loneliness, self-loathing, hatred, terror, desperation, and their kin haunt the inner rooms of the soul of anyone who has been overpowered by painful experiences.

The uniqueness of your circumstances and the emotional specters lurking within your heart do not need to be compared to anyone else's experience. Common ground is found in realizing you are not the only one who has preserved a sense of safety by learning not to feel too much.

PERSONAL EVALUATION

Look carefully at the emotional realm to discover if you hold a guarded vigil against emotions rather than have the ability to fully experience emotional health, or if you use emotions to manipulate and control others. The following lists are markers of what is emotionally healthy. Try to be specific in terms of what is uncomfortable for you.

Rate yourself on a scale of one to ten (one indicates that the statement is never true of you, and ten indicates that the statement accurately reflects your emotional condition on a regular basis) for each item.

Current Emotional Health   Rating

1. Able to feel, express, and accept the entire spectrum of emotions (sadness, happiness, fear, anger, jealousy, envy, and their various manifestations). . . . .   _____

2. Able to accept expression of the entire range of emotions in others, especially your children and spouse. . . . . . .   _____

3. Respond with emotional intensity appropriate to the situation (as opposed to overreacting or not feeling anything when it would be normal to feel something). . . . .   _____

4. Attach the emotional reaction to the true source (as opposed to transferring your emotional intensity to someone who did not prompt your emotions and does not deserve your intense emotional reaction; for example, blowing up at your child when you are angry with your spouse but feel unable to express your anger to your spouse). . . . . . .   _____

5. Able to enjoy what is joyful in the current moment (without obsessing about what might happen to snatch the joy away). . . . .   _____

6. Allow others to feel whatever they are feeling without having to take responsibility for causing their emotions or needing to try to change what they are feeling to make them feel better. . . . .   _____

7. Able to experience intimacy with persons close to you; to share deeply from your heart; to reveal your strengths and weaknesses; to accept their self-revelations, strengths, and weaknesses. . . . .   _____

8. Able to relate comfortably with others who are different from you (age, social status, financial status, education, and so on). . . . .   _____

9. Able to grieve your losses and move beyond them. . . .   _____

10. Able to trust when trust is warranted. . . . .   _____

11. Able to talk about feelings and to have feelings proportionate to what you think you feel. . . . .   _____

12. Able to visit symbols or mementos of past pain without being emotionally devastated or numb. . . . .   _____

13. Able to comfort others, being compassionate rather than controlling or judgmental. . . . . _____

14. Able to be alone without being overwhelmed with loneliness. . . . . _____

15. Derive pleasure from reality (of past, present, and future hopes) rather than from fantasy that is out of sync with reality. . . . . _____

Emotionally Nourishing Choices   *Rating*

1. Willing to take responsibility for your own emotional health even if you are not responsible for what caused the pain. _____

2. Ask for what you believe will help you feel better, and keep asking and seeking until you find what you need. . . . . _____

3. Take actions that lead toward emotional health and balance. . . . . _____

4. Remove yourself from relationships and situations that are hurtful to you over and over again in the same ways. . . . _____

5. Do for yourself those things that were neglected in your childhood. . . . . _____

6. Stop doing to yourself those things that have caused you pain and continue to cause you pain. . . . . _____

7. Develop relationships with persons who love and respect you as a valuable human being. . . . . _____

8. Make choices, commitments, and plans that lead to emotional health and healing of emotional wounds. . . . . . . _____

9. Admit when you cannot resolve emotional problems, and seek appropriate help until emotional balance is restored. _____

10. Participate in a network of people committed to giving and receiving emotional nourishment. . . . . _____

Dealing with Emotional Pain of the Past   *Rating*

1. Acknowledge, share with someone supportive, validate, and treat hurts and emotional wounds so they can heal. _____

2. Identify and grieve losses. . . . . _____

3. Resolve unforgiveness, bitterness, and resentment. . . . _____

4. Acknowledge the true facts of happenings that hurt you; end denial (of the who, what, when, where, and why of your emotional wound). . . . . _____

5. Reexamine beliefs about yourself and life (formed in reac-

tion to past abuse, deception, neglect, or victimization) in
light of adult understanding. . . . .   ____

6. Challenge old beliefs and replace them with beliefs that
affirm your true value as a human being. . . . .   ____
7. Express, analyze, and understand repressed emotions. . .   ____
8. Establish new symbols to remind you of the truth about
your value and your life. . . . .   ____

ACTION

For emotionally nourishing choices, pick the top three that you feel would best help you at this time. Consider each one as follows. Cite a time when you made that choice and what the results were. List how your current situation could be improved by making such a choice and what seems to keep you from making this choice.

In dealing with the pain of your past, pick items on the list you deem most important to resolve the effects of your past on you now. Write about the most glaring item from your past that has not yet been dealt with in that particular way.

REFLECTION

• What feelings don't you allow yourself to feel?
• How do you suppress emotions?

Beliefs and Assumptions

Your belief structure is a key player in developing codependent behavior. Your mind developed beliefs and assumptions you could use to gain a sense of security in the face of danger. Perhaps you believed if you were a better student or if you made yourself useful and relieved some of the pressure at home, Dad wouldn't drink, or Mom wouldn't fly into a rage.

You established beliefs that gave you an illusion of control over the danger of life. You drew conclusions about what left you vulnerable, then used them to determine what you could do to try to make sure you were less vulnerable. Once you established beliefs about what you needed to do and be, you devised rules to keep you out of the danger zone: creating a false image, obeying rigid rules (don't talk, don't trust, don't feel), observing superstitions, trying to be perfect, manipulating, and/or yielding to an abuser. The beliefs that helped you survive then may hurt your relationships now.

The problem is that when beliefs are established from a child's perspective, they are not based on reality. In reality, what you were taught about life may not have been right or true. In reality, neither were you responsible for nor could you have controlled the people around you. What was done to you had very little to do with the kind of person you are but much to do with the kind of persons you were dependent upon: their conditions, addictions, and compulsions.

Here's an illustration. Young Beth fell and injured her head. The experience was terribly frightening. In the hospital emergency room she was snatched from the arms of her mother. Under glaring lights, a man in a mask held her face. Another man plunged a large hypodermic needle into her forehead, then he took a needle and thread, sticking the needle into her flesh time and again. She heard them say they were giving her stitches.

Two years later, Beth visited her mother immediately following the birth of another child. At the family birthing center siblings were welcome to attend the birth. However, the nurse asked her to leave so she could give the mother stitches. Beth was horrified. She decided she had to do something to make sure she never again had to get stitches.

For the next few months Beth refused to eat meat. Her parents were concerned, but they didn't confront the issue. Finally, she said to her mother, "Mommy, I really would like to eat meat again, but I just can't! You told me that I need to eat meat so I can grow up to be strong and healthy. And if I grow up, I will have a baby. And if I have a baby, they will give me stitches again. And I made up my mind. I am going to make sure no one ever gives me stitches again!"

In her sincere attempt at self-protection Beth had given up something she enjoyed. She sacrificed a part of her life on the altar of an erroneous belief.

In hopes of protecting yourself, you may still be living by beliefs that needlessly deprive you of intimacy, trust, church, friendships, good feelings, rest, peace of mind, and the like. You may seek to control, manipulate, rescue, and fix others in the belief that you will ensure your security. The tragedy is that controlling others is not possible, and it holds no power to ensure security. Life is not, nor will it ever be, completely within your control. You can know greater hope of security by reevaluating beliefs foundational to your codependent behavior and challenging them.

PERSONAL EVALUATION

- What do you believe you have to do to protect yourself from being hurt again?
- What do you believe you can do to guard your heart from the uncertainties of life and the unpredictable behavior of others?

ACTION

Write a story from the perspective of the child within you, using the following lead sentences: The most overpowering experience of my life was . . . ; In order to survive, I believed that I had to . . . ; I thought that I could keep the danger of being overpowered again away if I would . . . ; In order to stay safe, I gave up . . . ; In order to stay safe, I tried to control . . . .

Make a list of beliefs you developed to help you feel safe. (For example, if I am a good person and always try to do what is right, bad things won't happen to me. If I never open up to anyone or trust anyone, I will not get hurt. If I don't express my feelings or let them surface, they can't hurt me.)

REFLECTION

Consider your emotional safety rules in these terms:

- Do they work for you as you assumed they would?
- What do you think you were reacting to when you developed these beliefs?
- Are these beliefs sound?
- Reexamining them from an adult perspective, which ones need to be changed?

ENCOURAGEMENT

When you change your beliefs, you will change your life.

FOOD FOR THOUGHT

We should be careful to get out of an experience only the wisdom that is in it—and stop there; lest we be like the cat that sits down on a hot-stove lid. She will never sit down on a hot-stove lid again, and that is well; but also she will never sit down on a cold one any more.

—Mark Twain

Mental and Intellectual Life

You could say that your intellectual capacities were the brains behind Operation Survival or Operation Striving to Please. You must have figured out a fairly good way of coping to become a person others depend on when they are in need.

PERSONAL EVALUATION

Below are some indicators of a healthy mental and intellectual life. Consider to what degree they represent your life and in what specific ways you are missing out on enjoying full mental and intellectual health.

Rate yourself on a scale of one to ten for each item on the following list (ten describes you most of the time; one means that you never think this way).

Indicators of Mental and Intellectual Health   *Rating*

1. Aware of and accept reality. . . . .   _____
2. Open to new ideas and willing to consider new information to refine beliefs; continually learn and grow. . . . .   _____
3. Able to balance rational understanding of life with emotional, physical, and spiritual realities. . . . .   _____
4. Aware of reasonable limits and seek to live within them (don't believe, "I can do anything!" but acknowledge, "I can do anything within my realistic limitations"). . . . . .   _____
5. See life as a continuum between two poles rather than all-or-nothing, black or white, perfection or failure; have self-image that is not grandiose or self-negating. . . . .   _____

6. Able to direct thoughts and imagination in healthy ways rather than be consumed with worry, fears, and obsession with the lives of others. . . . .   ———

ACTION

Pick three items rated five or lower that trouble you, and list specific examples of how your life is negatively affected by each.

Turn each problem area around into a desire for a healthy use of your mental and intellectual capacities to help you gain power over codependency.

REFLECTION

If your intellect is the brains behind your personal security system, you may find this exercise threatening. These new ideas may be rightfully disturbing to old ways of seeing yourself and life. Write down any feelings touched by this exercise, and describe why you think this exercise may stir up defensiveness.

ENCOURAGEMENT

The same mental and intellectual abilities you used to survive whatever threatened to overpower you in the past can be used to work toward gaining power over codependency.

Spiritual Life

Patterns of codependent belief and behavior are often carried over into spirituality. Today you will look at how codependency may manifest in your spiritual life. You will look at markers of healthy spirituality to see where you are missing out and consider common spiritual problems associated with codependency. In so doing, you will identify areas of spirituality you may want to take hold of as well as spiritual problems you may choose to correct.

PERSONAL EVALUATION

Consider these signs of spiritual health, and note to what degree they are part of your spiritual experience. Also note if you have neglected, avoided, or refused participation in any particular spiritual pursuit.

Rate your spiritual health on a scale of one to ten for each item listed (one means that you do not have this experience at all; ten means that this is a regular part of your spiritual experience).

Signs of Spiritual Health   *Rating*
 1. Secure in God's everlasting love for you. . . . . ____
 2. Confident there is a purpose and plan for your life. . . . ____
 3. Able to rest in the knowledge that your relationship with
    God is founded on love rather than dependent on your
    ongoing performance. ____

4. Able to trust God to take care of you and your loved ones. _____

5. Able to follow through on spiritual disciplines (prayer, meditation, worship, sharing your faith, studying Scripture, obedience, and so on flow from an internal desire to know, love, and please God, not from an external demand to maintain God's favor). _____

6. Experience the peace that comes from within and remains with you even during trying circumstances. . . . . _____

7. Acknowledge your need for God; don't assume God's need for you. . . . . _____

8. Able to receive forgiveness (can admit sin, failings, errors, willful acts of rebellion) and extend forgiveness to others. _____

9. Live in accordance with your personal faith, having words and deeds that correspond. . . . . _____

10. Practice humility rather than present a list of spiritual credentials; admit when you fall short rather than pretend to be perfect. . . . . _____

Spiritual Problems Associated with Codependency   *Rating*

1. Have poor relationship with God. . . . . _____

Either you don't think you need God at all, or you regularly confuse yourself with God. You may have cut yourself off from God for a number of reasons. Perhaps you blame God for not protecting you from whatever overpowered you. You may have concluded that God can't be depended on in times of need and that the only person you can really depend on or trust is yourself. Or you may have a grandiose view of yourself, often feeling responsible for the very survival of others. You may believe that if you do not intervene in the lives of those you love, rescue, and try to control, they will self-destruct. You have taken on the role of God in their lives. Another variation is believing that you alone know God's will for others, and it is your responsibility to enforce God's will upon them or manipulate them into obeying God. You sincerely doubt that God's will can be carried out if you don't see to it personally.

2. Tend toward hypocrisy, legalism, and self-righteousness. _____

You feel that you must maintain a "spiritual" image of perfection because you do not want God to get a bad reputation (since you are His personal representative) or because you believe your standing with God is based on the ability to perform to a standard of perfection. Therefore, you strive to live by the letter of the law. When you discover a flaw within, you cover it up (by pretending or by lying outright). You may also see yourself as being on a higher spiritual plane than most people (because you follow rigid religious rules) and console yourself for your imperfections by being judgmental of those who are "much worse than you are."

3. Create a god in your own image. . . . .   _____

Within the twelve-step and recovery traditions there is deep respect for reliance upon God "as you understand Him." That can pose a trap. You may unconsciously understand God in a way that fits with what you believe you have to do to survive. For example, if you grew up believing that your appearance and performance earned you acceptance, you may assume that God demands outward ritual and legalistic performance. God "as you understand Him" may be an idol fashioned in the likeness of your conclusions about life. If your understanding of God includes having to perform to continually appease Him, following superstitious rituals in an attempt to manipulate God's favor, requiring perfection and self-sacrifice whenever you fall short, God "as you understand Him" may be an enlarged version of the demands you already place on yourself. If your religion is a burden you bear, which does not supply nourishment for your soul, consider whether your view of God may be made in your own image.

4. Go to extremes of religious practice. . . . .   _____

At one extreme you may become addicted to religious practice; on the other you may see yourself above needing to participate in religion (I don't need to pray or attend religious services the way other people do; I find God within myself).

5. Have a compulsion to control God and the spiritual lives of others. . . . .   _____

You feel compelled to know precisely what persons in your life must do to please God, see it as your God-given responsibility to get them to comply, and take on the weight of their eternal destiny as though it were in your hands. You may feel compelled to analyze each situation, decide the best course of action, and use prayer as a wrestling match in which you attempt to gain control of God to get Him to do what you know should be done.

ACTION

Try to identify what stands between you and spiritual health. List any experiences that cause you to resist or neglect developing this dimension of your life. Do something today to move in the direction of greater spiritual health: read a psalm, say a prayer, sing a hymn, or speak with a minister.

For each spiritual problem that applies to you, describe specifically how it manifests in your life.

REFLECTION

- What do you think would happen if you let go of control in the spiritual realm of your life and the lives of others and left everything up to God?
- What do you think would happen if you invited God to reveal Himself to you as He is?

Financial Life

Today you will consider your financial life. Finances are a tangible limit. An objective examination of how you deal with finances will show you what you value, how well you take responsibility for your life, and areas where you may try to control others.

PERSONAL EVALUATION

Go over these items that are accepted as being part of responsible financial behavior. Note what is left undone. If there is a general category listed and you can identify an action that you neglect, be as specific as you possibly can.

Rate your financial health on a scale of one to ten for each item (one means that you do not do this at all; ten, that you do it regularly).

Place a check next to any area that you do not handle responsibly on a regular basis. (Note: You will probably find that much of this seems ridiculously obvious. However, that is precisely the point. When something prevents you from caring for your life in a basic way, it possibly indicates something more than appears on the surface.)

Normal Financial Responsibilities	*Rating*
1. Live within a realistic budget.	_____
2. Know current assets and debts; keep a running account.	_____

3. Plan for financial security in anticipation of possible cash-flow problems. . . . .   _____

4. Maintain checking account and regularly balance the figures. . . . .   _____

5. Spend only available funds. . . . .   _____

6. Develop skills and use abilities to be gainfully employed.   _____

7. Have clearly defined personal goals and priorities that guide the prudent use of finances. . . . .   _____

8. Able to provide basic necessities for self and dependent children through work or accessing available resources. . .   _____

Possible Financial Indicators of Codependency   *Rating*

1. Feel guilty whenever buying something for yourself. . . .   _____

2. Feel guilty whenever buying something at full price. . . .   _____

3. Spend discretionary income on others while your legitimate needs are left unattended. . . . .   _____

4. Feel guilty or unable to order what you really want while eating out and instead order something inexpensive. . . .   _____

5. Spend or gamble money indiscriminately (since you believe there will never be enough to get what you need anyway).   _____

6. Go without things you need even though you have the money to pay for them. . . . .   _____

7. Avoid getting medical care for yourself because you don't want to spend money on yourself. . . . .   _____

8. Consider spending money on your needs and wants to be a waste. . . . .   _____

9. Feel that you have to apologize, hide, or make excuses for anything you get for yourself, especially anything nice. . .   _____

10. Say that you don't care about having nice things as long as the others in your family do. . . . .   _____

11. Avoid fulfilling your earning potential because you can't conceive of spending money on yourself and you don't want the responsibility of deciding where to spend the money. . . . .   _____

12. Spend compulsively on things to make yourself look presentable to the outside world. . . . .   _____

13. Feel covetous and envious of anyone who has more than you because you feel your worth is judged by what you have, how you appear to others, and the externals of life.   _____

14. Pretend to have more than you do and disguise the reality

of your financial situation because you believe what you
possess reflects your true value in the world. . . . . . .   ⸻

15. Rigidly control the finances of others or use money as a
tool to manipulate others. . . . .   ⸻

16. Take on financial responsibility for others who should bear
the weight themselves. . . . .   ⸻

ACTION

Of the financial indicators of codependency that
apply to you, select the three that are most troubling, and describe specifically how they manifest
in your life.

Turn each problem into a statement of how you
want to change your life to correct the problem.

REFLECTION

* What feelings arose as you considered your financial life?
* What are you afraid will happen if you stop rescuing people who have become financially dependent on you?

Rediscovering Your Talents, Treasures, and Dreams

You are much more than the sum of your past. You are a unique human being, created by God with a unique purpose. Granted, you may not know yourself well enough to be familiar with your talents and treasures. You may have experienced such devastating disappointment that you dare not dream great dreams for your life. It isn't easy to take hold of your talents, treasures, and dreams when you are preoccupied with avoiding your inner life, guarding your heart from further injury, and pretending to be what you wish you were.

One important facet of gaining power over codependency is venturing into the uncharted waters of your unlived life. A fulfilling life is more than just recovering from the effects the behavior of others has had on you and reclaiming those parts of life you have been cut off from. Life, as it is uniquely expressed in you, must involve self-expression. *You* must choose and dare to live out your unique purpose and design.

Everyone has talents, treasures, and dreams. Talents are your inborn abilities. You may have a talent for art, music, athletics, mathematics, writing, dance, or drama. Perhaps your talent lies in mechanical abilities or relating to children. Talents can be developed but not acquired. Treasures are your favorite things—things you value for whatever reason or for no particular reason. A treasure is a treasure just because you appreciate it. Dreams are what you would wish for yourself if you dared. A dream is an emotional investment in what you would hope for yourself if you allowed yourself the privilege of hoping. Dreams hold tremendous power when they are the vehicles that let you envision yourself into a healthier way of life.

If you grew up in a dysfunctional or addictive family system, your talents, treasures, and dreams were probably discounted or even forbidden. When life is consumed with surviving, there is little done to nurture the heartfelt desires of a child. You can give yourself permission to pursue your talents, treasures, and dreams, even if no one else ever has. Gaining power over codependency involves living beyond recovery; it is choosing to live to the best of your abilities, regardless of what has happened to you.

PERSONAL EVALUATION

- What talents do you have?
- What do you treasure?
- If you were to dare to dream, what would your dreams be?

ACTION

List at least three talents you think you may have.

List ten things you treasure (possessions, experiences, foods, events, books, ideas, or anything else that is an expression of your personal taste).

Describe one of your dreams that has yet to come true.

Choose one talent to develop, one treasure to enjoy, and one dream to pursue. Commit yourself. Do something to move toward your talents, treasures, and dreams.

REFLECTION

Your talents, treasures, and dreams can lie dormant for your entire life if you do not take action to develop, experience, pursue, and enjoy them. Will you dare to develop your talents? Will you choose to give yourself the gift of enjoying your treasures? Will you risk pursuing your long-lost dreams? If you don't, no one—not even God Himself—will do that for you.

ENCOURAGEMENT

There is so much more to life than guarding your heart! There is so much more to you than the pain you are dodging! Make your recovery the start of a new life as well as the reclamation of a broken one.

Becoming Familiar with a Brighter Future

You are more than a recovering codependent. Your life consists of what is yet unrevealed and what is painfully familiar to you. You are more than an adult child of your parents, even if they were alcoholic or dysfunctional. Yes, maybe you are an adult child of alcoholics (ACA), and you should acknowledge how that still affects your life. It's good to recognize the effect, attend meetings, read books, try to understand and recover from the pain of the past. Certainly, it is essential to reclaim what is missing, face what has been avoided, and fill up the deficits if you can. But don't stop there. Dare to discover areas of your life left unexplored. Venture into new experiences and opportunities.

Envision your life as having been bombed out by the effects of another person's behavior. You may start recovery thinking that an enormous bomb crater is the most distinguishing landmark on the landscape of your soul. Codependent behavior might be seen as avoiding that part of your life so that no one knew a bomb had been dropped there. Recovery might be seen as filling in the crater so that the ground is level again. But your goal is more than recovery; your goal is to live a full life. Living a full life means recognizing that there are seeds of greatness in every human being, and that includes you. Find those seeds, nourish those seeds, and let a beautiful, healthy tree grow in the place where the bombs once fell.

To grow a new life out of the devastation of your past, whatever that may be, you must become familiar with new areas of life. You have had a lifetime to become familiar with your family's particular brand of chaos. Is it any wonder that when you are left without other input, you gravitate toward chaos? By becoming familiar with recovery principles, you have probably felt the power of the familiar at work there, also. You begin to see all of life as it relates to the recovery principles you are learning and the steps you are taking. As you attend meetings you relate to people who seem to understand what you have been through. They seem to know how you feel. They share common beliefs, and you gain a sense of belonging, which gives power to your recovery efforts.

There is a danger, however, that if you grow comfortable in the familiarity of recovery circles, you may find your life revolving around the pain of your past and your identity being defined in terms of what you are recovering from rather than who you are. It's fine to curl up in the cocoon of the recovery community as long as that is a transition into becoming a butterfly and emerging into a beautifully transformed way of life.

If you desire a brighter future that is markedly different from your past, you must familiarize yourself with a better life so that the power of what is familiar will draw you forward. Keep reading your recovery materials, keep attending the meetings that support your recovery, but don't deceive yourself into thinking that you don't need to take the time to face the pain in your life. Take all the time you need to work through the issues that have taken a lifetime to develop. However, at the same time begin to familiarize yourself with the beauty and richness of life that you have missed along the way. You must educate yourself, associate with self-respecting people, find mentors you want to emulate, tour model homes, read books about the kind of life you have never experienced as well as what you are coming out of, and expose yourself to cultural experiences that expand your appreciation of the beautiful. Startle your senses with good sensations!

PERSONAL EVALUATION

- What are some healthy, beautiful, rich parts of life that you have never been familiar with because you have been so focused on avoiding your past or recovering from it? (Think in terms of what you may have envied in the lives of others, what you have felt deprived of, what you always wished for or were attracted to.)
- Have you cut yourself off from one of your senses or from a specific part of life?
- What would it mean for you to enjoy the goodness you have missed while you were trying to avoid what reminded you of the pain?

ACTION

You are going to make a plan so that you can familiarize yourself with a brighter future. I highly recommend two tape series by Zig Ziglar: *Goals:*

How to Set Them, How to Reach Them and *Success and the Self-Image.* They are available through direct mail from the Zig Ziglar Corporation at 214-233-9191. Read *Living a Beautiful Life* and *Living Beautifully Together* by Alexandra Stoddard. These two books are guides to self-pampering and gracious living. They detail the positive side of life that is opposite the neglect of self-care, which is the codependent way of life.

Go to a library or bookstore today, and get a book that will familiarize you with a brighter future.

Order one of the suggested tape series.

Make a list of things you can do in the future to open your mind to a better way of life; include a reading list of books that describe the kind of life you wish you could have.

REFLECTION

Give yourself thirty minutes to daydream or imagine a brighter future in glorious detail. Try not to make this a fantasy escape that is completely disconnected from where you are. Find a way to start where you are and dream of the real possibility of a better life.

Accepting Full Responsibility for Your Life

To gain power over codependency, you must be willing to accept full responsibility for your life. That means accepting all of life, good and bad. It includes accepting yourself as you are: your true feelings (good and bad), your character (saint and sinner), your body, your beliefs and opinions, your brilliance and weaknesses, talents and treasures, likes and dislikes, victories and losses. It includes accepting the truth of your history, the reality of this moment, and your ability to learn, grow, and change in the future. It includes your ability to turn your life over to a Higher Power who can lead you into a new life.

As long as you hold on to the hope that someday, someone is going to ride up on a white horse and rescue you from your problems, you will never have a full life. God has given you access to the resources and abilities you need to rescue yourself. You may have been someone else's victim in the past, but if you refuse to take responsibility for solving your problems today, you continue to victimize yourself. Learning to rely on God involves drawing enough strength from your faith to solve your problems courageously.

Here is an illustration of what it is like to accept full responsibility for your life. Patrick is a restaurant manager. When he comes on duty, he accepts full responsibility for successfully managing the entire restaurant in a way that will uphold the company's high standards. He is responsible to perform his duties well, but he is responsible for much more than that. He takes care of problems and manages the effects of what others do within the restaurant. If a server offends a patron, it is not Patrick's fault, but it is his responsibility to be aware of what happened and accommodate the guest. If the steward fails to order enough food, it does no good to blame someone for the shortage; he must take action to get the food needed before they run out. He doesn't do all the work himself, but he accepts the responsibility of finding others who are capable of doing the work, delegates the duties, and makes sure everything gets done in keeping with the standards he has committed himself to uphold.

You are responsible for your life in similar fashion. As an adult, you are responsible for taking care of problems, setting limits on what behavior you will tolerate, and making sure your needs are met. You are responsible for managing the effects of what happens in your life, even though what happens in your life may not be your fault.

You also need to accept your losses. Some things in life are irretrievable. No one can give you back your innocence once it is obliterated. No one can give you back the love and nurturing you should have received as a child if you were neglected or abused. A twelve-step program is wonderful for dealing with addictive/compulsive issues, but working your twelve-step program cannot restore what you have lost. You must accept and grieve the losses. Once you accept your irretrievable losses, you are free to establish healthy relationships within the reality of the moment.

PERSONAL EVALUATION

- Are you able to acknowledge the good and bad parts of your life and yourself? (Many codependents see themselves as alternately all good or all bad. It is a sign of health when you can accept that you are an integrated person who is good and bad, just as those you try to help are both good and bad, weak and strong.)
- Are you willing to accept full responsibility for your life, even though you may not be at fault for much of what you become responsible to take care of?
- Are you willing to accept your losses and learn to grieve them so that you can move beyond loss to a better life?

ACTION

Commit yourself to accept responsibility for whatever facets of your life you are willing to accept at this time. Sign your initials after each area you are willing to accept responsibility to care for:

Physical life _____   Mental and intellectual life _____
Spiritual life _____   Beliefs _____
Emotional life _____   Financial life _____

Take some time to identify your losses and allow yourself to grieve. I suggest reading *The Grief Recovery Handbook: A Step-by-Step Program for Moving Beyond Loss* by John W. James and Frank

Cherry. There are grief recovery support groups throughout the nation. To locate one in your area, contact the Grief Recovery Institute and Healthline at 1-800-445-4808.

REFLECTION

Taking full responsibility for your life will allow you to begin solving your problems and moving beyond your losses. In each area of your life you will have problems to solve and losses to grieve. These problems and losses hurt you and may be at the heart of what intimidates you to the point that you have found it easier to focus on others. Accepting personal responsibility gives you power to reclaim the missing pieces of your life and begin to live fully. Carefully consider each area of life, and choose the one where you first want to start the work of reclaiming your life.

Facing Off with Fear

Fear and controlling behavior go hand in glove. Hidden within most attempts to control others is an element of fear. Of course, we may not appear to be afraid. That's the beauty of a glove. It insulates the hand within, and it also masks the appearance of what is concealed. Your controlling behavior may come across as confidence, competence, righteousness, love, concern, "only trying to help," and a host of other images; but the force beneath the surface is often fear. You may recognize your fears most notably when people are out of your control; when they are late getting home, you discover they are not where they are supposed to be, or you detect dishonesty. If at these times you imagine catastrophe and worry obsessively, if you have already attended their funeral or rehearsed their murder, fear has its grip on you.

If you are to gain power over codependency, you must face off with fear. You must dare to look beneath the image to find what you are so afraid of. You can diffuse fear of its power, but to do so, you must recognize when controlling behavior is rooted in fear and the veiled need for self-protection.

Your controlling behavior may seem reasonable in obviously fearful circumstances. If you are in a relationship with a violent drug addict, it makes sense to try to prevent the person from using and becoming violent. However, there is a hidden fear as well. What is the fear keeping you in such a relationship? Could it be that fear of rejection, fear of losing your self-image as the rescuer, or fear of realizing no one else would have you keeps you in bondage?

One woman who facilitates a codependency support group confided that she did not gain power over codependency until she unmasked her real fears. She said, "The turning point came when I realized how selfish my rescuing and controlling behavior was. When I tried to get treatment for my alcoholic son, covered up for him, or tried to control his behavior, the real motivation was that I couldn't bear for anyone to know *my* son was in such a condition. I pretended to offer help for his sake when I was afraid of what people would think of me. I couldn't curb my urge to control his life until I faced off with my deepest fear: being rejected by my peers." Her identity was tied up in her image. If she took her hands off the situation, she might lose her son and risk losing her identity.

Rich and Becky's marriage had survived major difficulties. Rich was raised in a rigidly controlled home where his mother's emotional needs threatened to smother him. When he finally broke away to begin his own life and marriage, he was tired of being controlled. Yet he married Becky, who was controlling, only in new ways. Rich responded with passive-aggressive patterns he had learned in his family of origin. Several years into the marriage Rich revealed he was struggling with homosexuality and had broken their marriage vows by acting out sexually. He was willing to seek treatment for sex addiction since he wanted to save their marriage and did not want to live a homosexual lifestyle.

Becky and Rich were able to work through the crisis during inpatient treatment. Thereafter, the greatest challenge for Becky was to resist trying to control Rich's thoughts and actions. She constantly wanted to know what he was thinking, if he was feeling tempted, where he was, who he was with, and so on. This behavior triggered Rich's old feelings of being smothered, which were part of the downward spiral of his addictive cycle. Rich took responsibility for remaining faithful to his marriage vows in spite of his struggles. Becky took responsibility for facing her fears and releasing control of Rich's life to him. Both maintain their commitments one day at a time.

Fear uses the power of your imagination. Zig Ziglar says that if you try to battle your imagination with your will, imagination will win every time. The only way to win a battle with your imagination is to use your imagination.

PERSONAL EVALUATION

Think of specific times you try to control the lives of others. Ask yourself what you are afraid would happen if you didn't control the person or situation. Look beneath the surface to deeper fears that may motivate your behavior.

Recall any scenes you play in your mind or worry about when the other person is out of your control. What catastrophes do you imagine? What benefit do you get from worrying?

ACTION

List everything you are afraid might happen that triggers your controlling behavior. Note persons you try to control, what you are afraid might happen, and what you are afraid that would mean in your life.

Create a personal survival plan to cope realistically with what might happen. Carry the catastrophe all the way through until you have envisioned a way to survive your worst fear in a healthy way. Imagine what you would do to deal with the pain, what you would do to find replacement for what you risk losing (whether that is social standing, possessions, or your relationship). Research and plan specific action to care for yourself and minor children. Get phone numbers, names of professionals, and so on.

Work on your plan until you feel confident that regardless of what others choose to do with their lives, you have a way to go on living in a healthy way. Know exactly who you can turn to for help, how you will get where you need to go, and how much money you will need to take care of you until you are safe. Begin taking steps to save enough money, and prepare the practical arrangements that would be necessary to get you through the possible crisis and lead to a better life for you.

Once you have imagined, researched, and prepared your worst case survival plan, put it away in your notebook in the section on living your life. It is there if you ever need it. In the meantime, choose to allow others to live their own lives.

REFLECTION

Now that you have planned for the worst, you are free to hope for the best. You have the power to choose how to use your imagination. You are free to use it to imagine that your spouse or loved one is late because of doing something constructive, just as you can use it to worry that your loved one is acting out the behavior that has hurt you in the past. Think of a time when you worried or obsessed over another person's life and those worries turned out to be unfounded. Imagine other positive scenarios until the facts reveal whether you have anything to worry about.

Once you have seen yourself surviving the practical and emotional difficulties that threaten you, you will be less compelled to control the other person.

Processing Guilt and Condemnation

In codependent relationships, guilt, condemnation, and self-condemnation often get mixed up together in overwhelming proportions. Overcoming codependency involves sorting out condemnation from true moral guilt, refusing to accept the condemnation, and processing valid guilt in a healthy way.

You establish a codependent relationship on the basis of your self-concept that says you are able to fix or transform another person. When the relationship gets under way and the person fails to progress as you planned, the tension of unpleasant feelings and failings prevails.

You confront the person with the failings. Condemnation and blame get tossed back and forth. A person with healthy self-respect could let the condemnation pass. But in a codependent relationship, when condemnation is served up, you feel the need to run to meet it. Your partner knows where you feel inadequate and uses your insecurities as a way of alleviating personal guilt and responsibility for actions that are wrong or out of control. Instead of refusing the condemnation, you accept it and turn your attention toward trying a little harder to be what the person wants you to be. Your willingness to try to change to accommodate the other's weaknesses reveals a level of self-condemnation in you.

When you choose to stop codependent patterns of relating, you must be willing to admit that you cannot be or do all you seemed to promise when the relationship began. You must reestablish the relationship with new rules of play, particularly that you will not accept responsibility for the other person's feelings or failings. You will no longer accept the condemnation that says you are to blame for the person's choices. You will no longer entertain self-condemnation that says when the person relapses or does anything wrong, something was lacking in you as a person.

True moral guilt occurs when you have done something wrong or you have neglected doing the right thing when it was in your power to do it. There is no basis for true guilt when you have done something right and someone else's feelings are hurt. The codependent response to a moral dilemma is this: Will my action upset the person or cause the person to act out the addiction in some way? The question you need to ask yourself is this: Is this behavior or choice the right thing to do? You are responsible for doing what you know to be right. You are not responsible for the interpretations and reactions of others to the decisions you make with a clear conscience.

To free yourself from condemnation, you must decide on your moral standards and be prepared to use them as your guide for when you will accept guilt or condemnation. Some people see the Ten Commandments or clear moral teachings in the New Testament as symbols of bondage. In reality, those clearly defined boundaries between right and wrong can bring you security. As long as you are willing to access the forgiveness available when you are wrong, those moral boundaries can act to point you in the direction of freedom from guilt. If you do not have clearly defined moral standards, you will never be free of guilt and condemnation. You will always be left waiting for someone else to define whether what you have done is wrong, and you will always be left wondering whether you need to apologize for something.

Here's how to live without wallowing in guilt and condemnation. Whenever you experience guilty feelings, stop to examine their source. *Condemnation* suggests there is something wrong with who you are, not with what you have done. Condemnation bids you to try to change to accommodate what someone else needs you to be. *True guilt* is experienced when you do something that violates your moral standards or violates a commitment that you entered into willingly.

When others try to dump condemnation on you and you have determined that you have not done anything wrong, don't accept it. Calmly, but firmly, explain that you are sorry they are upset because they think you should live your life differently, but you cannot always be what they feel they need you to be.

PERSONAL EVALUATION

Think of a specific time when you were willing to accept the condemnation someone served you because it played into your sense of inadequacy. For example, you grew up being told that you were not filling your mother's need for love. "If you were a good son, you would visit your mother more often," Dad says. Although you visit your mother regularly, you accept that there must be something wrong with you, and you reply, "I'm sorry. I've just been busy at work (or some other excuse). I'll try to get by more often." You mean: "I'll try to be a better son."

Think of a specific situation that makes you feel uncomfortably guilty at this time in your life. Try to sort out the true guilt from condemnation or self-condemnation.

ACTION

Define in writing your moral guidelines for what is right and wrong.

Consider the situation that is making you feel guilty. On a piece of paper, write three headings: "Condemnation," "True Guilt," and "Self-Condemnation." Sort out the situation in the following way. List statements that infer you are responsible for others' feelings or failings under "Condemnation." List anything you have done that violates your moral code under "True Guilt." List any feelings of personal inadequacy that cause you to be inclined to accept others' condemnation under "Self-Condemnation."

Process each column in the following manner.

"Condemnation"

Rehearse how you will decline accepting responsibility for their feelings and failings. Write a note that hands them back the condemnation and explains why you are not going to accept it or try to change to please them.

"True Guilt"

Clearly define where you have done wrong; admit it to God, yourself, and another person; determine how you will make amends. Then make amends as necessary.

"Self-Condemnation"

Consider the self-condemnation and accept that as a part of your current self-image. (You can choose to reclaim a healthy sense of self during your recovery, but it is not necessarily something you need to deal with at this moment.) List the relationships where your feelings of inadequacy in this area incline you to accept condemnation when it is offered.

FOOD FOR THOUGHT

No one can make you feel inferior without your consent.

—Eleanor Roosevelt

Establishing Relational Boundaries

Establishing relational boundaries involves drawing the line between your life and the lives of others. Gaining power over codependency means accepting full responsibility for your life and letting go of responsibility for the lives of others. Today you will determine where you cross the line into the lives of others and where you allow others to overstep the boundaries into your life.

Physical Life

You overstep others' boundaries whenever you try to control their physical behavior: what they do, how they choose to do it, where they go, when they go, and so on. Certainly, when you are married to someone, you need to draw definite boundaries regarding what type of behavior you will tolerate. That has to do with establishing your boundaries. You can choose what the consequences will be if the person's physical actions are unacceptable to you, but you cannot control what the person does.

Emotional Life

You overstep others' boundaries whenever you try to control, fix, or assume responsibility for how they feel. That includes trying to make them love you, make them happy, or make them sorry for what they have done.

Spiritual Life

You overstep others' boundaries whenever you take responsibility for spiritual life: playing God in their lives, convicting them of every little sin, dictating God's will for them, or using spiritual manipulation, such as trying to "put the fear of God into them."

Mental and Intellectual Life

You overstep others' boundaries whenever you think for them, speak for them, or try to solve their problems instead of allowing them to figure things out for themselves with your support. You violate their intellectual boundaries whenever you insist that your way is the only right way, insist on giving unsolicited advice, and act as though they are accountable to you for what they decide to do.

Financial Life

You overstep others' boundaries whenever you take responsibility for their financial irresponsibility: allowing them to live in your home without holding down a job or contributing income, covering bounced checks so that the family reputation is not tarnished, allowing them to continually borrow money when they refuse to pay back what has previously been borrowed, and so on. Trying to control their financial habits or manipulate them by bribery of any sort falls into this category.

Next you will consider how others may overstep the boundaries into your life and where you will draw the line.

Physical Life

They overstep your boundaries whenever they endanger your physical well-being, threaten to do bodily harm, invade your privacy, or force you to behave physically or sexually in ways unacceptable to you.

Emotional Life

They cannot overstep your emotional boundaries without your involvement. They truly cannot make you feel any particular way, but their lives invade your emotional boundaries whenever you carry their burdens, feel their feelings instead of holding on to what you feel at any given time, or worry over things you have no power to control in their lives.

Spiritual Life

They overstep your spiritual boundaries whenever they require you to stifle your spiritual life to make them feel more comfortable. Outsiders may violate your spiritual boundaries by suggesting that you are partially responsible for another person's spiritual condition just because you are in close relationship. Whenever you bear the weight for others' spiritual lives or sins, your boundaries are violated.

Mental and Intellectual Life

No one can make you think in any particular way unless you agree to continue in mind games. Their lives encroach on your mental and intellectual boundaries whenever you change your opinion or beliefs to try to be accepted by them, whenever you are consumed with trying to figure out how to solve their problems, whenever you read a book and find yourself thinking more in terms of how it relates to them than how it relates to you, and so on.

Financial Life

They overstep your financial boundaries whenever they take away your financial security or rely on you to provide more than your fair share in a given circumstance or whenever they violate financial commitments they have made to you, such as not paying back a loan as promised.

PERSONAL EVALUATION

- Select one person whose life seems enmeshed with yours, someone with whom you need to establish a "No Trespassing Contract."
- Consider each of the following areas of the person's life: physical, emotional, spiritual, mental and intellectual, and financial. Define specifically how you cross the line in each area.
- Consider each of these areas of your life, and define specifically how you allow the person to trespass in your life.

ACTION

Commit yourself to release responsibility for whatever facets of the person's life you are willing to release at this time. Sign your initials after each area you are willing to release (whether or not the person accepts responsibility to care for it):

Physical life _____   Mental and intellectual life _____
Spiritual life _____   Financial life _____
Emotional life _____

Make it your goal to stop trespassing in the person's life. Commit yourself to acknowledge every time you overstep the boundaries; confess this fault to yourself, another person, and God; move in the direction of trespassing less as you grow in your recovery.

Decide if you are willing to allow the person to continue to trespass in your life. Decide what behavior is unacceptable to you and what you are willing to do about it. At some point, communicate what your boundaries are, what you intend to do to protect them, and what you will do if your boundaries are violated.

ENCOURAGEMENT

Establishing boundaries and observing them bring security and respect to all relationships. This step is worth your effort.

Finding Strength to Change

You will need strength to carry out your recovery plan. However, if you have the strength it takes to behave in a codependent manner, you already have the strength to gain power over codependency. You simply have to learn to apply your strength to your personal problems.

Here's a story that illustrates this point. A woman called a radio talk show complaining that she didn't know how to handle her situation. She was married to a very nice man, who had a drinking problem. The family, including five children, depended on him for the major part of their finances. Her husband's drinking was a regular part of life, but she said she had managed to "work around" it so it didn't affect the children. Every year or so, her husband would leave unexpectedly and call her from the Bahamas where he had friends and could escape the pressures of family life. Sometimes he would be gone a week, sometimes for months. This time he told the children he would be out for an hour and called a week later to say he would be back in three more weeks.

The woman was calling the talk show host in hopes of finding out how she could keep from getting angry. (So far she had been able to maintain a loving attitude in hopes that it would help her husband not feel so pressured and need to escape.) She also wanted to know how she could persuade him to change since nothing she said about his need to stop drinking and stay home had any impact. The show's host rightly pointed out that she was in denial and suggested she was using her strength ineffectively. It took a tremendous amount of strength for her to maintain a loving attitude when she was suppressing her rightful indignation at her husband's behavior. It took strength to pretend that everything was fine when it wasn't, to continue to convince herself that she could work around her husband's alcoholism and abdication of responsibilities, so her children were not affected. The host told her this unacceptable behavior would continue as long as she was willing to put up with it and until she began to use her strength effectively.

Whatever your situation, it takes tremendous strength to protect yourself from the pain of the past, to continue living without those parts of your life that are missing, trying to adapt yourself into someone you believe will be able to cure someone else, exerting rigid controls over your feelings, environment, and people you love.

Dr. John C. Maxwell quoted Fred Smith as saying, "A problem is a problem if I can do something about it. If I cannot do something about it, it is a fact of life." These are facts of life: you cannot control another human being's temperament, addictions, conditions, behavior, and so on. When you use your strength to solve what is not in your power to solve, you divert yourself from doing things you can do something about. The woman in the story and many who develop patterns of codependency get the equation backward. They exhaust their strength trying to solve facts of life while expending their remaining strength trying to live with their problems and deny their feelings.

To gain power over codependency, you need to own your real feelings, separate your problems from the facts of life, and then use your strength to solve the problems and reclaim your life. The best you can do with facts of life is to face them, accept them, and decide how much you are willing to allow them to affect your life in the future. Then set boundaries in terms of how much you are willing to take.

PERSONAL EVALUATION

- How do you waste your strength by trying to suppress, deny, or ignore your true feelings? trying to solve, change, or deny facts of life? trying to learn to live comfortably with your problems?
- Are you ready to use your strength in a new way to gain power over codependency?

ACTION

List three personal problems you are willing to use your strength to solve.

List the facts of life you now live with (your loved ones' addictions, conditions, choices, and so on).

Define where you draw the line. How much will you allow their lives to affect you before you take action? What will be the consequential action you take if they cross the line?

REFLECTION

The Serenity Prayer has been used by many people as a step toward sorting out their problems from the facts of life. Pray the prayer and remain quiet for thirty minutes. Reflect on what can and cannot be changed in your life.

God, grant me the serenity, to accept the things I cannot change, the courage to change the things I can, and the wisdom to know the difference. Amen.

ENCOURAGEMENT

You have had to be strong to survive. You can direct that strength to give you power over codependency.

FOOD FOR THOUGHT

It takes as much strength to actively ignore a problem as it does to solve it. It takes more strength to try to change the facts of life than to face them and learn to live in spite of them.

Dealing with Your Past

In considering the various parts of your life that are missing or damaged, you may realize that your life has been deeply affected by the behavior of others, which you had no power to control. Although you cannot control others, you can control your attitude and actions in response to their effect on you.

If you had been born into a poor family in London of 1891, you might have made the best of a bad situation by becoming a chip seller. London's streets bustled with activity. The morning commute brought some twenty thousand horse-powered vehicles over London Bridge, carrying gentlemen and ladies, merchants and artisans on their way to transact business in the city. London's odors were as loud as the hooves clacking on the cobblestone streets, as more than forty thousand horses also stopped to do their business in the city. Gentlemen in top hats made their way across the sullied streets, while the poor made a meager living sweeping dung from their path in hopes of receiving a coin or two. Boys, known as chip sellers, would follow, using pans and brushes to collect the manure, which they sold for fertilizer in upper-class neighborhoods.

The chip sellers' response to the manure around them can be used as an allegory of what you can do with the effects of others' behavior that has soiled your life. Everyone has been dumped on, at one time or another.

When you let people into your heart, you cannot help being affected by their lives. Sometimes that includes dealing with messes they make. What makes the difference in life is what you do with those messes. Some people who grow up in the stench of painful and abusive relationships have never seen themselves unsoiled. They identify with the manure, assuming that is what they are. Some people disconnect from it and discreetly step around the truth of their past and the effects it still has on them today. They are often perceived as hypocritical and self-righteous as they try to distance themselves from anything that smells of their past pain. Others just sit in the mess, stir it up, and complain about how unfair life has been. They don't make a move to get out of the way of another load. They just play the martyr, curse the injustice, and use their pile of misery to excuse their own nonachievement; they wallow in it.

Here is a healthy approach. Recognize that there is an unpleasant mess and that it is not of your making. Instead of avoiding it, look at it, and deal with it. See beyond the disgusting appearance and foul odor. Chip sellers recognize that there is value in the emotional and relational manure of life. They see it as fertilizer from which new life can grow. Melody Beattie says, "A codependent person is one who has let another person's behavior affect him or her, and who is obsessed with controlling that person's behavior." In gaining power over codependency, you must learn to recognize where the behavior of others has affected you, whether or not you let it happen; you take ownership of the effects in your life and turn them into something from which new life can grow. That means learning to deal with the effects that have already been dumped into your life in a way that hastens your healing and works to your benefit.

The obsessive attempt to control is connected to feelings of powerlessness when you were unable to protect yourself from pain others brought into your life. If you were hurt by others when life was out of your control, is it any wonder that you feel more secure when life (any part of life) is under your control? Your desire for security is understandable, but the means you have chosen to maintain your feelings of security simply don't work. They also sabotage healthy relationships with persons closest to you.

Cleaning up the messes of your past and dealing with them positively will bring you the greatest level of security. You will gain power by learning how to use these experiences to enhance your personal growth. During the remainder of your journey, you will be shown how to do just that. Whether you choose to do so is your responsibility.

PERSONAL EVALUATION

Consider your current situation and the negative effects of others' behavior that you have to deal with. To what degree did you allow yourself to be in a position to let this happen? (For example, did you choose a relationship with a person you knew had an addictive/compulsive condition? Were you ignorant or intimidated so that you were rendered powerless to escape? Were you deceived, being taken by surprise with the consequences of hidden addictive/compulsive behavior?)

How are you dealing with it? Avoiding the effects? Wallowing in the mess, seeking pity, or using it to excuse not living your life fully? Trying to control others so you feel protected? Or are you processing the effects in a way that enriches your life?

ACTION

You are going to deal with the messes of your past so that you can develop your plan for new life. Make four columns across the top of a page in your notebook: "Who?"; "What?"; "What Effect?"; and "Power Level?" Down the left margin, write your age in increments of five years: 0 to 5 years, 5 to 10 years, 10 to 15 years, and so on to your present age. For each age group, list everything you can recall that had a memorable negative effect on your life due to the behavior of others. When were you hurt and who was responsible? Include when people did things they should not have done and when they failed to do things they should have done. Summarize these in capsule form. Who? Mom. What? Drunk. What effect? I had to take care of siblings. I went through an emotional nightmare. Power level? Rate the amount of power you felt you had at the time over what was happening to you (one means that you felt absolutely powerless, and ten means that you felt you had enough power to stop the negative effects on your life).

Consider all the significant people in your life during each phase. Have you not dealt with messes from your past relationship with them? Do not exclude people just because they have died; their effect may not be dead in your life. Fill as many pages as necessary, trying to limit your time spent to one hour. Your goal is to catalog the ways the behavior of others had a negative impact you had to deal with. You are not trying to heal every wound or even cope with the issues raised. You are simply making a catalog for future use.

REFLECTION

Feelings may emerge that seem dangerous. Accept the feelings as valid, given what has happened in your life. Acknowledge how you honestly feel, identify where the feelings originated (which phase of your life), and express your feelings in some tangible nondestructive way. You may choose to write, talk to a supportive friend, pound your pillow, or cry yourself to sleep. Whatever you honestly feel or don't feel is O.K.

DAY
23

Developing Your Recovery Plan

One reason that finding power over codependency can be so baffling is that codependent behavior is symptomatic of a host of unresolved issues and erroneous beliefs. Dealing with codependency as though it were a single issue would be like a child trying to fell a flock of birds with a single stone. Codependency is a "flock" of issues that tend to fly together in lives of people who have lived in situations where their well-being was out of their control—most notably homes where drug addiction, alcoholism, or other dysfunctional systems took their toll.

Today you will construct the format for your personalized recovery plan. You will learn a process for resolving the effects others have had on you, reclaiming your life, and allowing others to live their lives. It will be up to you to pursue the help you need to deal with each issue as it applies in your life. The process looks like a continuing cycle.

The missing parts and problems of your life are symptoms of what fuels your codependent behavior. First, identify the symptom. Second, identify the obstacles and emotional injuries that cause you to miss out on that part of life (hurt, loss, shame, fear, guilt, blaming others). Third, identify your problems (what you can do something about) related to the issue. Fourth, reframe your view of

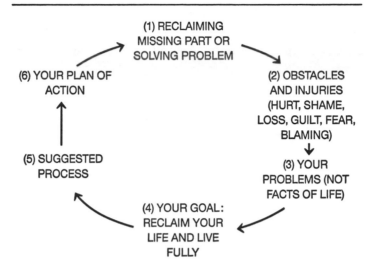

(1) RECLAIMING MISSING PART OR SOLVING PROBLEM

(6) YOUR PLAN OF ACTION

(2) OBSTACLES AND INJURIES (HURT, SHAME, LOSS, GUILT, FEAR, BLAMING)

(5) SUGGESTED PROCESS

(3) YOUR PROBLEMS (NOT FACTS OF LIFE)

(4) YOUR GOAL: RECLAIM YOUR LIFE AND LIVE FULLY

each problem into a goal. Define what you want to reclaim for your life and what you want to pursue in life once your problem is solved. Fifth, for each issue there is a suggested process to consider. Consider the suggested process and choose how you will implement it. Sixth, devise a specific plan of action to reach your goal. You will know that you have accomplished the goal when the original symptom is no longer a problem. If your plan of action does not seem to be working for you, reconsider the suggested process and try a different approach, or use different resources until you reach your goal.

Today you will clearly define your goals. All you have to do is to look back over the exercises you have already completed and choose what you are willing to take action on at this point in your life. You will obviously not be able to resolve all the issues you have identified as priorities. Select a few goals to focus on initially. Then as you successfully achieve them, you can replace them with new goals.

When you have power over codependency, you have a positive balance in these three areas: (1) resolving the effects the behavior of others has had on you, (2) living your life fully, and (3) letting others live their lives. You will be setting goals in each of these primary areas.

PERSONAL EVALUATION

Review Days 9, 10, 11, 12, 13, and 14. Pick the one area missing from your life that you want to reclaim or one problem you want to solve.

Review Day 15. Pick one of your talents or dreams to develop or pursue.

Review Day 20. Identify the one person with whom you most need and want to establish a "No Trespassing Contract."

If you remain committed to improving in all three areas and taking steps in those directions on a consistent basis, you will experience ongoing power over codependency.

ACTION

Earlier, you created three sections in your recovery notebook: "Effects," "Live," and "Let Live." Put eight sheets of paper in each section, following the sheets describing your selected goals, and label them: (1) "Missing Part or Problem," (2) "Goal," (3) "Benefits," (4) "Obstacles and Injuries," (5) "Knowledge/Skills Needed," (6) "Resources of

Knowledge/Skill," (7) "People/Groups/Organizations That Could Help," and (8) "My Chosen Plan of Action."

"Effects" Section

On page one, identify the missing part of your life that you want to reclaim or the problem area you want to resolve. On page two, turn this around into a goal of what you want your life to be like when you reclaim the missing part or solve the problem. On page three, list all the benefits you will experience as a result of achieving your goal.

"Live" Section

On page one, identify what you think has kept you from developing your selected talent or pursuing your dream. On page two, state the talent you want to develop or the dream you want to pursue in terms of a goal. On page three, list the benefits you will experience from developing your talent or pursuing your dream.

"Let Live" Section

On page one, name the person with whom you want to enter into a "No Trespassing Contract," and describe the problems caused by trespassing in the person's life and allowing the person to trespass in your life. On page two, clearly define your goal for not trespassing or allowing trespassing in terms specific enough that you will know if you are staying within your goal lines. On page three, list the benefits to you of maintaining a "No Trespassing Contract."

In each of these sections leave pages four through eight for later use.

REFLECTION

- Think about what you really want when you set out to deal with each item you have selected.
- Envision how your life will be different once you achieve your purpose and accomplish your goal in each area.

ENCOURAGEMENT

Codependency is a "flock" of issues and problems that fly together. By setting your sights and clearly defining your goals aimed at dealing with specific "birds" in your flock one at a time, you will discover the power to eventually bring down the whole flock.

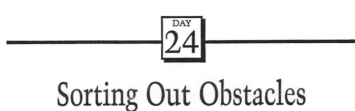
Sorting Out Obstacles and Injuries

There must be some obstacle or injury that causes you to avoid, neglect, or refuse to take responsibility for those parts of your life that are missing. There must be some reason you neglected your talents or abandoned a long-lost dream. There must be something that makes you feel more comfortable taking care of or trying to control others instead of caring for yourself, some reason you allow others to trespass in your life. The only way you will be able to develop a whole and healthy life is to identify which obstacles and injuries hold you back, then deal with them on your way to achieving your goals.

Imagine that your life is represented by a house. In your house is a closet crammed full with those parts of life that you have been missing. You busy yourself in other rooms filled with important activities and people who need you. You dare not open the door of the closet for fear of being overwhelmed. So far, your journey could be compared to daring to open the closet door, pulling everything out, and selecting a few items to keep out. Everything that had been out of sight and out of mind is before you in a conceptual pile. When you look at what has been missing, you know it is too important to throw away (you might need it someday), and yet you may not know where it belongs, why it was stuffed away, or how to deal with it.

You have also identified areas of life that you rigidly try to control. These are not items within the closet. They represent the ways you stand outside the door and put your weight against it to make sure it stays closed. Your rigid attempts at control of your emotions, environment, or other people are the ways you have learned to protect yourself from whatever is hidden in that closet. Once you learn to deal with the issues associated with the items in the closet and the closet is in order, you won't need to stand guard at the door; thus, the compulsion to exert rigid controls will dissipate.

Don't give in to the temptation to stuff everything back in the closet and close the door. You need to categorize each item, learn what to do with each group of items once they are sorted out, and realize that you don't have to deal with all the issues at one time. I will give you conceptual boxes and tell you how to determine what goes into each one.

PERSONAL EVALUATION

Here are the conceptual boxes. Since we are dealing with issues of human life rather than things, a neglected part of your life may be associated with more than one category; itemize it in all categories in which it fits.

The Hurt Box

Include anything associated with emotional injury. Whenever you have been wronged, by life or by another person, the experience leaves a painful remnant or splinter in your soul. A child with a splinter in her hand will cry, "Don't touch it! It will hurt!" Anything missing from your life that triggers a "Don't touch it!" response when you get close to it goes in the hurt box.

The Loss Box

Include anything associated with a loss of any kind: a job, self-respect, freedom, trust, beliefs, money, innocence, possessions, health, friendship, roots, a sense of security, death, or divorce. Another form of loss involves the things that someone should have done for you, the things that you missed out on. Perhaps your parents neglected your basic needs, and you kept waiting for someone to take care of you as you should have been cared for and to show you love by filling up a deficit in your life. You may have left some things undone because you are still waiting for the love that you missed to suddenly appear. These are things you balk at doing for yourself because it feels like closing the door on the possibility of someone, someday, loving you as you should have been loved as a child.

The Shame Box

Include anything you feel the need to hide or keep secret, anything associated with pretending in order to be accepted, anything you don't do because you feel unworthy or undeserving, anything you consider too expensive although you have the money, anything you cannot imagine asking help with (out of fear of exposure), anything excluded or not tried because you think something wrong with you disqualifies you, or anything you can't talk about.

The Fear Box

Include anything that arouses fear: fear of rejection, fear of the consequences, fear of someone else's reaction, fear of abandonment, or fear of letting go of control.

The Guilt Box

Include anything associated with guilty feelings: if you feel guilty for not doing it, assume you would feel guilty if you did do it, or feel condemned by others for doing or not doing it.

The "Blaming Them" Box

Include anything you do not do because of others, their expectations of you, their dependence on you, or what they might do if you did this. Anything missing from your life associated with blaming others or using them as a reason or excuse for your failure to act goes in this box.

The Practical Box

Include anything you don't do for practical reasons, such as lack of resources, conflicting commitments, and actual limitations based in reality.

ACTION

Read over the pages "Missing Part or Problem" and "Goal" in all three sections of your notebook. As you do, carefully consider each one to see if it is associated with any of these boxes. On the page "Obstacles and Injuries" in each section, list every box that you think may be associated with an obstacle or emotional injury that has impaired your life and keeps you from achieving that particular goal.

Let me give you an example of how this works. Emily, the woman who entered treatment in reaction to her husband's addiction, realized that she had a problem with buying anything nice for herself, especially sleepwear and underclothes. She always dressed well for work, but when she began scrutinizing what was missing from her life, she made an unusual discovery. She did not own any socks other than the stockings she wore to work. She wore her daughter's socks or her husband's socks. That was a missing piece Emily set out to reclaim. In her notebook she wrote: "Missing"— Nice socks just for me; "Goal"—Figure out why this is something I neglect and buy myself an assortment of pretty socks.

In sorting through the emotional boxes associated with the symptom of the socks, Emily discovered she had experienced injuries to her feet that were left untended as a child in a chaotic home. Her father worked in a machine shop and left metal shavings throughout the house. She was allowed to go barefoot, and she lived with this painful symbol of neglect. For this issue she checked off the boxes for hurt, loss, shame, fear, and blame. She started to check off the practical box because she told herself that she couldn't really afford to waste money on socks for herself, but she caught herself and erased that one. On the page "Obstacles and Injuries" she wrote: hurt, loss (Daddy is never going to take care of my feet or buy me pretty socks), shame, fear, and blame. She recognized these issues as having caused her to shy away from this tiny part of life that reminded her of the physical and emotional pain of her past.

REFLECTION

When you clean out a closet, you empty it, consider the items, categorize them, and decide what you want to reclaim at the moment. The items left are stored away, in organized fashion, for easy access when you are ready to use them. For now give yourself permission to put away all the other parts of your life that you have not chosen and accept that you can deal with the rest later.

ENCOURAGEMENT

Help is available to deal with your obstacles and injuries. Once you identify the issues, you are well on your way to being able to overcome the obstacles and begin healing the injuries.

Reaching Out for Help and Support

You may need to be persuaded to reach out for help. After all, you are probably the one who usually dispenses help to others. You may feel quite comfortable being needed but quite uncomfortable admitting your needs and seeking support for yourself. I would venture that there are some parts of your life where you shine, particularly the parts you have given your attention. However, you are not dealing with those parts of life on this journey. You are dealing with the parts of life you have been cut off from. In these areas you will need help to achieve your goals and support to maintain a new life-style.

Suppose you awaken during the night to find that you have slept on your arm and the circulation has been cut off from that part of your body. You are awake, but your arm is "asleep" and you want a drink of milk. Assuming that any adult should be able to handle the simple task of getting a drink, you go to the kitchen. You reach for the milk carton, you think you have a good grasp on it, but the feedback going to your brain from the part of your body that has been out of circulation is distorted. Although you think you have a good grasp on it, the carton slips from your hand. The realization strikes you that until circulation is fully restored to that part of your body, you can choose not to use it, or you can have someone help you do the things you need to do, not only to get the circulation going but also to take hold of what you are reaching for.

The parts of your life you are dealing with now have been out of circulation. They are still "asleep," even though you may be remarkably capable in other areas of life. You may assume that since the goals you are focusing on during this journey are simple tasks any adult should be able to handle, you can do this by yourself. But the feedback coming back to you may be distorted. You may think you have a good grasp on some issue, but you can't figure out why you can't hold on to what you are seeking. One reason you may have been cut off from this part of your life could be that you didn't want to ask for help and you couldn't handle it on your own. You need help in two ways: help to get the circulation going to these parts of your life again, and help in reaching toward your goals once you reclaim the parts of your life you have been cut off from.

Support Groups

When you are involved in an ongoing process of growth, you need support and encouragement. Your ability to maintain a new life-style will be positively affected if a small group of people knows your aspirations and will hold you accountable to stay on track. These people should care for you, understand the issues you are dealing with, share your values, and be willing to press their lives into yours in an affirming way. Get support that builds up your family. However, all of your support should not come from within the immediate family. You can benefit greatly from having access to a group that can help you reflect objectively on your life from outside your family system.

Some support groups are established with specific themes, such as Adult Children of Alcoholics, Incest Survivors, Codependents Anonymous, and Al-Anon. There are also support groups for spouses of persons attending various twelve-step groups for their particular addictive/compulsive behavior.

Whenever you are trying out a support group, commit yourself to attend for at least six weeks to allow yourself and the other group members to get a sense of relationship. If you don't like a particular group, try another one.

Counselors

A therapist who specializes in dealing with codependency or with your particular issues can be a tremendous help. You need to find someone you can grow to trust, a person with a reputation of helping others who shares your values. Just because you once went to a counselor who failed to be of help, don't discount all counselors. If you go to a counselor who does not help you, find someone who can.

To find a good counselor, ask people you trust to suggest someone. You can request meetings with prospective counselors to determine if you feel confident in their ability to deal with your issues. Most will do this free of charge. Ask what their philosophy is in relation to your issues. If you don't feel comfortable with them or with their approach, ask for another referral. Don't be hesitant to shop for the person who will be able to agree with your values and help you. This important matter is worth researching until you are confident in a counselor's ability to help you. Beware of disqualifying counselors just because they focus attention on painful areas of your life. Pain is a part of the healing process in recovery as it is in physical surgery.

Inpatient Treatment

People who deal with codependency rarely seek inpatient treatment unless there is a severe crisis in the family. They usually cannot afford the time away from life because so many people depend on them. If a crisis tears you away, consider inpatient treatment as a way to accelerate your recovery. You receive skilled professional help to face your deeply buried issues, and you also have the time and privacy to deal with things that you would probably not feel comfortable dealing with while carrying your daily responsibilities. Treatment programs are not all alike. Make sure the values and philosophy of the program are in keeping with your own.

PERSONAL EVALUATION

- Are you willing to reach out for help and support in reclaiming the parts of life you have been cut off from?
- If not, what is your reason?
- To whom can you turn for support as you gain power over codependency?
- To whom are you willing to make yourself accountable in terms of continuing to move forward in your recovery?

ACTION

List the names of the people who act as a network of support for you, and describe one way each encourages your continuing pursuit of gaining power over codependency.

List the pros and cons of seeking professional help. Decide if this is something you want to pursue.

On page five of each section of your notebook, make a list of the help you think you need to gain knowledge and skills to help yourself.

On page seven of each section of your notebook, make a list of the individuals, groups, and organizations that could help you cope with your issues and achieve your recovery goals.

REFLECTION

How have you grown over the course of this journey to be able or willing to reach out for help and support?

ENCOURAGEMENT

There are people who can offer genuine help and understanding for your issues. Don't stop looking until you find them.

FOOD FOR THOUGHT

Two are better than one,
Because they have a good reward for their labor.
For if they fall, one will lift up his companion.
But woe to him who is alone when he falls,
For he has no one to help him up.

—Ecclesiastes 4:9–10

Identifying Resources

Tremendous resources are available for every imaginable facet of recovery. Once you have identified specific goals and objectives, you can find resources to give you the knowledge you need, help you develop the skills you want, and provide practical assistance and support. Listing many specific resources here would not be beneficial since each person taking the journey is focused on individual goals. I want to give you some ideas about how to track down resources.

You probably have access to more resources than you could ever exhaust just working through your local library and your telephone directory. Here are the steps to finding resources in any area of interest.

Step One

Identify the area where you need help or more information. (You have already done this.)

Step Two

Check at your local library for books on the topic or related topics. You can go to the card catalog (a file of cards that represents every book available through the library). The cards are listed by topic and by author's last name. Most libraries have a variety of books on recovery issues. Ask a librarian to recommend some books on the topic or guide you to the section of the library that holds the books you need.

Step Three

Contact organizations set up to deal with issues related to your area of interest. A great resource for family-related issues is Focus on the Family. You can call them and receive leads about almost any conceivable family issue. The telephone number is 719-531-3400. Your local Alcoholics Anonymous group can usually direct you toward twelve-step groups and Al-Anon groups.

- Another way to track down groups and organizations is to use your telephone directory. Look under city, county, state, and federal governments for numbers of agencies. If you are not sure that a particular agency can help you, call and explain what information or help you are trying to locate. Staff persons will usually know where to direct you if they cannot help you.
- A growing network of treatment centers and recovery groups has resources available. You can contact counseling offices, treatment centers, or universities and usually get leads about people, groups, and organizations that help individuals in specific ways. There is also a growing network of recovery bookstores. Locate one in your area, and ask the proprietor for leads to resources for whatever help you need.
- You can call the offices of radio talk shows. Radio talk programs have to keep an extensive listing of guests who address various topics. They

will probably have a list of referrals to groups, reputable counselors, and organizations as well.
* The best resources are human resources. Within your community, there are church groups, men's groups, women's groups, recovery groups, parenting groups, educational seminars, and so on. To tap into these meetings, you can contact your local Chamber of Commerce.

The real key to finding information and resources is to keep on seeking, keep on asking, and keep on knocking. Once you know what you want to accomplish, what tasks you need to complete to reach your goals, what information or help you lack, it's just a matter of persistent effort to track down the resources.

PERSONAL EVALUATION

What are three things you can do today to track down the information you need to reach your goals?

ACTION

Do those three things!

In your notebook in each of the three sections, compile a list and keep track of the resources you have located that move you toward your goal.

REFLECTION

* How far did you get in finding the help you need?
* Are you encouraged or discouraged by the process of actually reaching out toward your goals?

121

ENCOURAGEMENT

There are tremendous resources available to help you work through your issues. Don't stop looking until you have the resources you need to recover.

FOOD FOR THOUGHT

Ask, and it will be given to you; seek, and you will find; knock, and it will be opened to you. For everyone who asks receives, and he who seeks finds, and to him who knocks it will be opened.
—Jesus Christ

Give Yourself Some Time

Transforming your life constitutes a major project. Just because recovery seems monumental does not mean that it is unreachable. You merely need to give yourself some time. You can approach it in the familiar way most Americans purchase a home or a car. You do it on the installment plan. You calculate and negotiate the cost (what you need to do to deal with your accumulation of issues), clearly define your commitment, break down the payments into amounts you can afford, spread out the payments over a manageable span of time, and enter into a binding agreement by making a personal commitment. When the commitment is sealed, you begin to live in the house or drive the car, even though ownership is not yet completed.

It's the same with recovery. You can figure out your options, break down the recovery action plan into manageable amounts that are within your reach at the moment, and spread out your recovery plan over the course of moments, days, weeks, months, and years to come. Carefully consider what you need to deal with to live your life freely, weigh your decision, define precisely what you are committing yourself to do, then seal the commitment with a binding agreement.

You can begin to live with power over codependency today by staying within the limits you have defined and by relying on the support system you arrange. You will continue to make payments (taking the actions you have committed yourself to, such as reading, attending support groups, seeking treatment or counseling, making nourishing emotional choices, and so on) on a schedule as you have committed yourself to do. You would also do well to have someone to whom you make yourself accountable to continue to make these payments.

Give yourself some time each day to nourish yourself and care for yourself in tender ways. At first you may not know what to do with time reserved just for you but make a commitment to give yourself at least an hour a day. You will discover the joy of finding out what nourishes your soul, what appeals to the child inside your heart, and what replenishes some of the nourishment you have been lacking.

Commit yourself to a block of time each week to review your recovery goals and pursue outside help. It might be making a weekly visit to a counselor, attending a twelve-step group or a seminar, or reading and discussing books related to the issues involved in your recovery. Review weekly how you are progressing in the three areas that constitute gaining power over codependency: resolving the effects the behavior of others has had on you, living your life beyond mere recovery, and allowing others to live their lives.

PERSONAL EVALUATION

- Are you willing to set aside at least an hour each day to nourish yourself and a block of time each week to focus on resolving the issues that trouble you?

- Are you willing to make a long-term commitment to deal with the issues you have discovered during this journey so that you can reclaim your life and begin to live fully?
- Are you willing to allow someone you trust to encourage you and hold you accountable to continue making the payments necessary to live in recovery?

ACTION

If you do not already have one, draw up a written schedule of how you currently spend your time. Then rearrange your commitments so that you have reserved the time to continue making investments in your recovery and self-nurturing.

Put the specific commitment of time you are willing to make into writing along with your signature. Allow another person to witness your commitment, and ask the person to encourage you and hold you accountable to continue living in recovery.

REFLECTION

It has been said that time heals all wounds. That is not true! Time alone does not heal any injury, whether it is physical, emotional, or spiritual. Time used appropriately to take action that deals with the real injury brings about healing. If a wound is ignored and goes untreated, it will grow worse in the course of time. Your choice to give yourself some time to tend your wounds and nourish yourself is a very important one.

ENCOURAGEMENT

You can begin living in recovery today if you are willing to give yourself the necessary time and use it appropriately.

FOOD FOR THOUGHT

What wound did ever heal but by degrees?
—William Shakespeare

Life, Liberty, and the Pursuit of Happiness

We the people of the United States, in order to form a more perfect Union, establish justice, insure domestic tranquility, provide for the common defense, promote the general welfare, and secure the blessings of liberty to ourselves and our posterity, do ordain and establish this Constitution for the United States of America.

—Preamble to the Constitution
of the United States

We hold these truths to be self-evident, that all men are created equal, that they are endowed by their Creator with certain unalienable rights, that among these are life, liberty and the pursuit of happiness.

—From the Declaration of Independence

With these powerful words the American people are offered the opportunity and dignity necessary to live out their lives in freedom. And yet untold millions live in some form of bondage, without fully apprehending the life they have been given the right to live. No one—not government, society, your spouse, or your dearest friend—can give you anything in life that you will not appropriate for yourself.

Life, liberty, and the pursuit of happiness are yours for the taking, but only if you dare, only if you take the risks involved, only if you choose. You can use your freedom to overcome the effects others have had on you! You can venture to express and develop the life within you! You can pursue happiness! You can also respect the rights and responsibilities of others to do the same for themselves or, if they so choose, to abdicate those rights and responsibilities.

Just as the American system of government uses checks and balances, establishes and revises lawful boundaries, and delineates specific rights of the individual that deserve to be protected, you need to set up your own form of self-government that allows you to appropriate your own "life, liberty and the pursuit of happiness." You need to find a network of people who will check you and help you keep your life in balance by giving you honest feedback, encouraging your efforts at learning to take care of yourself and keep from trespassing in the lives of others. You need a group of people who will act as a legislative body to help you figure out where to set boundaries, how to enforce them, and when the boundary lines need to be changed. You need to develop for yourself some clearly defined rights that will protect and support you in learning to care for yourself.

PERSONAL EVALUATION

- Who can you rely on to help you keep your life in balance as you live out your recovery?
- How can you set up relationships so that they can provide the checks and balances you need to stay on track?
- Which individuals or groups could help you con-

tinually mark out the boundary lines for your life and the lives of others and will support you as you learn to enforce them?

ACTION

Write out the answers to the questions above and put them in your notebook on the page "My Chosen Plan of Action."

Make your own personal Bill of Rights, listing specific items you have deprived yourself of in the past that you will give yourself permission to claim.

You may hesitate to claim your rights. It may be difficult for you to say you deserve anything. That is O.K. If you have trouble making a list of rights, make yourself a growing "It's O.K." list. Write in your notebook each little item you want to reclaim that you have deprived yourself of in the past. Where you might feel dishonest saying, "I have the right to buy myself nice things," you can say, "It's O.K. to buy myself something nice occasionally." Add these to your list as you dare: it's O.K. to order steak instead of chicken; it's O.K. to take time to smell the roses; it's O.K. to say no when you don't want to do something; and so on.

The Harvest of a Healthy Life

In the Introduction, these questions were raised: Precisely, what is recovery from codependency? Is it vowing not to help other people who need you? Is it becoming totally self-sufficient so that you are not dependent on anyone else? Is it recovery from being too nice? How do you know if you have relapsed into codependency? Now is the time for you to discover the answers about where you draw the line between recovery and relapse in your life.

Early on in your journey you saw codependency depicted in the image of a tree. Now I will give you an illustration of what recovery from codependency looks like. The life of a person who has power over codependency can be represented by a tree. This tree is beautiful. Its great branches stretch toward the sky, providing shade for many who rest beneath it. The dense foliage is dotted with the brilliant color of healthy fruit growing from the branches. The tree is filled with sounds of birds, squirrels, woodpeckers, and a host of insects that make their home amidst the branches. If you look carefully, you will notice that the soil in which the tree is planted has been tilled and seems to have been cultivated with a rich supply of fertilizer. A small stream has been diverted to pass by the tree, so the roots have a continual source of nourishment to replenish the life of the tree.

Someone takes care of this tree on a regular basis.

The sun is shining down from above. It seems fine. The beauty, the busyness in the branches, and the coolness of the shade are attractive. The fruit is sweet. The tree itself is not wasting away from within; life flows in the tree and through the tree.

As your tree of life continues to grow, you schedule regular times of pruning the branches. Even though you temporarily inconvenience those who have nested there, you do this to sustain continued health of the tree. The fruit growing on the branches is the love and joy, peace and patience, kindness and goodness, gentleness and self-control beginning to emerge in the seasons of your life.

You draw the boundary line between recovery and relapse when you choose to live in a way that gives to others without inhibiting the nourishment and tending you need to remain healthy and fruitful. There are now limits to what you are willing to give or endure for the sake of others. When you choose to sacrifice of yourself, it is out of love freely given without demanding repayment. Your value, relationships, and security are still affected by your history, but you are learning to resolve those issues. Your identity is no longer just the rescuer, savior, martyr, or one who holds things together for everyone else. You are discovering who you are, beyond the definition of what you do for others. You are venturing to believe the tree of your life deserves a place in the world apart from its usefulness and appearance. You still fear that if you let go of control, you may not be safe and the people you love might leave you, but you have made contingency plans that enable you to live courageously in the presence of your fears.

PERSONAL EVALUATION

Consider how you have grown during this journey to gain power over codependency.

ACTION

Draw another picture of your life as a tree, illustrating how you have changed (roots, trunk, soil, branches, fruit, nourishment).

REFLECTION

Reflect on how your life is different and how you will continue to grow in this new way now that you have learned how to gain power over codependency.

ENCOURAGEMENT

You can resume giving to others and caring for others once you have established a life-style that also involves nourishing yourself, and once you have established boundaries that let you know when you are becoming depleted or when others are taking advantage of you.

FOOD FOR THOUGHT

Cursed is the man who trusts in man
And makes flesh his strength,
Whose heart departs from the LORD.
For he shall be like a shrub in the desert,
And shall not see when good comes,
But shall inhabit the parched places in the
    wilderness,

In a salt land which is not inhabited.
Blessed is the man who trusts in the Lord,
And whose hope is in the Lord.
For he shall be like a tree planted by the waters,
Which spreads out its roots by the river,
And will not fear when heat comes;
But its leaf will be green,
And will not be anxious in the year of drought,
Nor will cease from yielding fruit.

—Jeremiah the Prophet

Deciding Where You Go from Here

Although you have come to the end of the 30-day journey outlined in this book, your personal journey continues. I hope you recognize that you can gain power over codependency. Sure, you have unearthed areas of your life long buried that need continued attention, but every human life requires ongoing care. Now you are in a position to get yourself help and give yourself the care you need to give attention to those areas of life.

We have defined gaining power over codependency to mean balancing your resources and abilities in each of three areas: resolving the effects the behavior of others has had on your life, living your life, and letting others live their lives. As you continue to maintain a healthy balance in these areas, you really are experiencing power over codependency in growing measure.

Whenever you find yourself overindulging in the lives of others and their responsibilities, take a look at the list of issues in your life awaiting your concern. Select another one, and put your energy into responsibly caring for it.

PERSONAL EVALUATION

You have already taken decisive action to learn new things about each area. You have a notebook with goal sheets and forms to follow toward achieving your worthy recovery goals. Why stop now? Each time you achieve one of your goals in each area, choose another to replace it. In this way you will continue to grow and find a sense of confidence that comes from knowing you are moving in the right direction.

The important thing is not to lose momentum. Each day, one day at a time, keep your dreams clearly in sight, your goals well-defined, your boundaries marked out, your obstacles targeted for attack, and your relationships growing. The journey continues.

ACTION

Decide whether you want to go back and work through this journey again, now that you are familiar with the process.

Decide if you will continue to use your notebook to record and monitor your progress in gaining power over codependency.

Decide whether you are going to continue to follow a calendar or schedule that gives you time for dealing with your recovery issues and for nurturing yourself.

Forgive yourself for whatever you feel you didn't do well enough during your journey.

Make a commitment to continue moving forward and making positive choices to overcome whatever obstacles that may present themselves along the continuing road of life.

Reflection

- After taking your journey, do you have a greater sense of balance in all three areas?
- Are you taking clearly defined steps and making commitments to achieve balance in all three areas?

Encouragement

Walking in power over codependency opens you up to a whole new way of life. Keep walking, one step at a time, in the direction of recovering from the effects of others' behavior, living your life, and letting others live their lives. Enjoy your continuing journey!

Food for Thought

Character is the ability to carry out a good resolution long after the excitement of the moment has passed.

—Cabot Robert

For Further Reading

Beattie, Melody. *Codependent No More*. New York: Harper & Row, 1987.

Bradshaw, John. *Homecoming*. New York: Bantam Books.

Buhler, Rich. *New Choices, New Boundaries*. Nashville: Thomas Nelson, 1991.

———. *Pain and Pretending*. Nashville: Thomas Nelson, 1988.

DesRoches, Brian. *Reclaiming Your Self*. New York: Dell Publishing, 1990.

Murray, Marilyn. *Prisoners of Another War*. Berkley, Calif.: PageMill Press, 1991.

Springle, Pat. *Rapha's 12-Step Program for Overcoming Codependency*. Houston/Dallas: Rapha Publishing/Word.

If after taking *Your 30-Day Journey to Power over Codependency* you feel the need for further help, call New Life Treatment Center, 1-800-277-LIFE, for a free and confidential consultation.